IN LOVE AND WAR

IN LOVE AND WAR

A LETTER TO MY PARENTS

MARIA CORELLI

Introduction by Jason Goodwin

 SHORT BOOKS

First published in 2001 by
Short Books
15 Highbury Terrace
London N5 1UP

10 9 8 7 6 5 4 3

A CIP catalogue record for this book
is available from the British Library.

ISBN 1-904095-08-9

Printed in Great Britain by
Bookmarque Ltd, Croydon, Surrey

To my son Oliver

Author's note

The letter which follows is word for word as I wrote it in 1944 (some of the names have been altered to protect the identities of the people concerned). In places, the language might seem a little strange. This is because I was thinking in Italian only, and had forgotten English – absolutely necessary under the circumstances.

Acknowledgements

DAME ALISON MUNRO, who was one of the first readers, who urged me to get it into publishable form and made many helpful suggestions.

JASON AND KATE GOODWIN, who got everything moving and encouraged me at every stage.

JO CORELL, who was so efficient and supportive in the typing and the processing.

MAX and MURIEL, my wonderful parents, who were always in my thoughts throughout my captivity, which inspired me to write this letter.

INTRODUCTION

More than 50 years have elapsed since *In Love and War* was written, without a title page, just an address in Rome, and the date. It was May 1944, Rome had just been liberated by the Allies, and an English girl who had gone to Italy before the war began was finally free to write home. The letter would break an anxious four-year silence, to explain her war, and its remarkable outcome.

The letter is published here for the first time. It is exactly as she wrote it, and if the English slips now and then, those slips are part of the story she has to tell, for four years living a dangerous secret life in wartime Italy had already transformed Mary into the Italian Maria.

The letter was sent to West Wittering, on the Sussex coast, where Mary was brought up in a house built by her father, the architect MacDonald Gill. The house stands hard by Chichester Harbour and looks out to East Head across the sands. Max's people were Chichester, and his brother, the sculptor and letterer Eric Gill, lived at Ditchling in the Downs.

In West Wittering, now, as then, there are long dunes

and fast tides. People mess about in boats. Children regulate the rippled sands. When the tide turns, the castles topple and a host of handkerchief yachts turn to the north, and come streaking in for tea.

In 1940 Mussolini pulled Italy into the war. The country was unprepared. The public were unenthusiastic. The military were inadequate. In Greece and North Africa, Italian forces had to be rescued by German intervention. While Mussolini traded the role of a European political giant for becoming Hitler's careworn stooge, his popularity at home began to wane. He sent Italians – quite unnecessarily – to the eastern front, and in December 1941 he ruinously declared war on the United States. By the beginning of 1943, North Africa was lost to the Allies, and when in July they began to take control of Sicily, Mussolini suddenly lost power. The King of Italy, for years no more than a figurehead, invited the dictator to an interview. Afterwards, as Mussolini was shown out, the royal guard stepped forward and arrested him. The King appointed an elderly admiral to be prime minister. Italians did not protest.

The way was now open for Italy to surrender, on 8th September 1943. Italian soldiers deserted their units. Allied prisoners were released from POW camps in the countryside, and started to make their way south, hoping to reach the Allies who were moving up ponderously through Italy to Naples. A month later, Italy declared war on Nazi Germany, so the war wasn't over, after all. German divisions were rushed south, and the country was put under German military command. Mussolini was sprung from his prison in a daring raid, and installed in a puppet regime in the north.

Then began the battle for Italy that the Italians had been dreading, between Germans, Allies and Italian partisans. Not until the Allies opened a second European front in Normandy in early 1944 did the German hold begin to loosen. Rome was liberated in June 1944. Mary Corell emerged from hiding, and took a job as a translator for the British High Command. On the embassy type-writer, she wrote the extraordinary letter which follows.

After the war Mary lived for a time in America. She became a couturier, and in the end she settled again in West Wittering, in a coastguard cottage by the sea. For forty years she was a certificated teacher of Scottish dancing in Chichester. At the same time she taught Italian, indeed she still does – total immersion – with such brio that for a while I thought she was Italian herself. Other students would mutter something about an exile from Mussolini's Rome. We knew her as Maria, of course: *Maria Corelli*. I picked up the idea that she was a grand Italian anti-fascist.

Exciting as it seemed, that fiction melts into insignificance when it is set against the true story she tells in *In Love and War*. Another writer might have laboured the coincidences and elevated the drama, but Mary at twenty something wrote everything down exactly as it happened. She kept the letter private until one day, at a party, she mentioned that she had a story to publish, and that she had waited half a century until *the people who were with her in the cave were dead*.

Mary's letter brings the news that after four years of total silence, locked away in wartime Italy, she is alive. She has left her husband, the nice Englishman, and taken up with a man who should have been dead by all the logic of that terrible war. But, at the level of the particular, the war has no logic. It has inconveniences that must be overcome, and dangers to be avoided. The Jewish baritone is released from concentration camp in Italy because the doctor says that damp is endangering his voice. An English couple stay on in Italy after war is declared and the embassy is withdrawn because the Italians agree that a singer should not break her training schedules. A girl may faint from hunger in a city full of friends; or wind up hiding in a cave. She may endure danger and privations without rancour, but hate her enemies for the way they stole her clothes. Her husband is arrested when a German officer, glancing through the window at a crowd of Italian peasants, recognises that one of them is an Englishman.

Meanwhile a Nazi officer, thinking to show his sympathies, muddles two names: he shoots the man he wants to save, and releases a man he has never met.

Every year or so Mary goes back to the south of Italy. About ten years ago, she was riding in a taxi when she found the driver scrutinising her in his mirror. Finally, he declared they had met before. Could it be – was it possible – that the signora had been in his little village during the war? Ridiculous, of course, but – Picinisco?

Jason Goodwin 2001

Maria Corelli, Rome, 1944

SOME OF THE PEOPLE, etc, IN THIS LETTER

Max (MacDonald Gill)	my father
Muriel (Gill)	my mother
Priscilla	my stepmother
Anne	my sister
John (Gill)	my brother
Lewis (Leslie)	my husband
Sigbert (Steinfeld, later Corelli – of which the anglicised version is Corell)	best friend
Rosanna	chief girl friend
Patrick	close family friend
South Nore	home in England
' Nonna'	a large piece of ham
Edgeworth & Nancy	Lewis's brother & sister-in-law
Diana Fawcus	school friend
Puck	a much loved cat

Via Vittorio Veneto – ROMA
Written between 4th July and 8th September 1944

My darling Max and Priscilla

Maybe this is the most difficult letter I have ever written because I have to tell you something very serious and perhaps you will say terrible and sad. It is very difficult to tell you, but I terribly need your comprehension and I ask you if possible not to judge me until we have been able to see each other and talk about it. I have left Lewis. You will be shattered by that and say – how is it possible? What has happened? Does Mary realise what she has done? I want to try and describe to you all our life of the last four-and-a-half years. (Perhaps I write stilted English now as it is much easier for me to think, speak and write in Italian than in English.) It is strange how one can even lose the habit of one's own language.

Well, when we were last able to correspond, it was spring and early summer of 1940. Do you remember what our life was at that time? We were living at Pensione Nella where we had a piano in our room, we were successfully studying singing with Signora Tamajo, and we already had a large clientele of English students, most of which I taught as Lewis needed time for composition and piano. We had one real and very great friend (whom you remember) Sigbert Steinfeld, an opera singer, who was in Italy singing and waiting for his visa to emigrate in America where his brother, a painter of whom you may have heard at the Paris Exhibition, Alfons Takal by name, is now an American subject. Sigbert lived only two minutes from us and we spent every day together. The evenings we would spend always in his room, he singing and Lewis playing. He has a beautiful baritone voice which gives complete happiness to listen to. Well, we were always together in our free time and all our interests were in common. Also it was he who introduced us to Signora Tamajo. (He has a sense of humour like yours, Max – I should say similar to yours)... It was right from the beginning in December 1939 when we first knew him [Sigbert] that I realised I loved him and it was soon after I realised that he loved me. You will say – 'how was it possible? But you loved Lewis so much – we *know* you loved Lewis from when you were 16 and that was as real as it could be.' Yes, that's what I thought. But it was possible, and I, who am not a changeable person, was cut off from Lewis almost in one day. The strange thing was that we did not feel we were wrong against Lewis. (You may say that is the feeling of a supreme egotist.) I was terribly happy with Sigbert. I lived every moment for him and he for me and yet at the same time the natural friendship between us three was not spoiled, neither did we feel when we were with Lewis that we were being hypocrites. I did not know whether Lewis imagined this or not and only a few weeks ago did I learn that he had seen it all from the beginning, but being convinced it was a kind of schoolgirl passion on my part that would end as soon as Sigbert left for America he said nothing. He did not know that if Sigbert had left for America even then I should have gone with him... So our life continued until the 10th June 1940; the day that Italy entered the war. I remember so well the atmosphere on that day. I was having a singing lesson, and almost by chance Signora Tamajo switched on the radio to listen to Mussolini's speech. Up till that moment I did not believe he would bring Italy into the war, and when I heard his words I was horrified. I got back to the Pensione as soon as I could, feeling sure that everybody in the street must know I was English. I remember the drear, lonely feeling in seeing the British Embassy closing up and leaving, surrounded by soldiers. That evening we three spent as usual in Sigbert's room but for the first time everything was darkened, and we leant out of the window in the dark discussing what our future might be – two English and one

Jewish ex-Romanian, who was born and brought up in Germany. Was there any hope for us to be able to continue our life as it was? After ten days came the answer. On the 19th, I went to Sigbert's room as usual at 2 o'clock and the landlady greeted me with tears in her eyes telling me that two policemen had come that morning, had arrested him and taken him she did not know where. You can imagine my desperation. Lewis and I spent that afternoon at the American Embassy trying to persuade them to trace Sigbert and get him sent to America as soon as possible. But it was useless – all foreign Jews had been arrested and nobody knew where they were. On the same day, as by a trick of irony — Lewis and I received a letter from the same Embassy saying that the Italian Government had decided to continue hospitality towards British subjects and they could continue living as before on condition that they lived quietly and avoided large gatherings of people. Those were terrible days. I could not reconcile myself to the absence of Sigbert – he seemed to be everywhere and yet I could not see him. I was terribly sad but tried not to let Lewis see it – he was always so good and kind to me. Every day I went to Sigbert's landlady and to Signora Tamajo to see if they had had news, and only some time later did the landlady receive a short letter from Sigbert saying that he had been in prison for three weeks but was now in a Concentration Camp in Calabria, south

Italy. He wrote only one letter to us and we only one to him, assuring each other of everlasting friendship which would not change even if correspondence was not possible. You cannot imagine what it is like living in a dictatorship country; especially in wartime – everything one did was dangerous – everyone you spoke to you had to imagine might denounce you the next moment. It was said that Fascists were never Fascist when single but became firmly so immediately when with two or three others. I was quite ill during those months and had to stop singing and English lessons till September. Lewis and I tried to piece our life together again; most English lessons fell off for the time being (anyway it was strictly prohibited to us to teach English – but we did so all through the war, for necessity) but we received a regular monthly subsidy from the American Embassy which enabled us to pay Pensione expenses and with what lessons we still had we paid for our singing and living. Very gradually and after some time I found I was able to return to Lewis and love him as before, though I could never in any way forget Sigbert, and many times I thought to myself that it was inevitable that I should love him for always. You will say, how is it possible you could love them both at the same time? Well, in those days it was possible. For the next year our life was very regular: singing lessons three or four times a week with Signora Tamajo, a few English lessons and our own life of quiet companionship at Pensione Nella, which consisted in every evening playing Racing Demon together, or reading or playing duets, or going to the cinema, and sometimes Lewis used to read out loud while I sewed or knitted. Lewis tells me now that those days were a poem for him. Our chief joy in the winter was going to the opera which we did at least once every week (starting also from when Sigbert was with us and we three went together). That as you can imagine is marvellous in Italy, and we enjoyed it more than anything. In the summer we often took the small electric train and went to Ostia (lido of Rome) even though we were not really supposed to leave Rome at all. Ostia is not by any means beautiful but for us, always living in the town, it had the advantage of sun and sea. We used to spend all day there taking our picnic with us. By then I could speak Italian fluently. I did not find it very difficult and spoke after about three months. For Lewis it was more difficult – he says he is not gifted with languages. We began making friends – Adele Puccini, an American girl (some distant relation to the composer) also studying music and later on singing with Signora Tamajo; and her fiancé Philip Callea, also American and a medical student of the University. Adele is rather a graceful, tall, dark girl, a little older than I, and Philip is rather an ordinary, narrow-minded type of little country doctor (really, we have never quite made out why they were engaged).

Then there was Mrs D'Andrea, an English woman married to an Italian. It was in February 1941 that we first knew Rosanna. Rosanna Moretti, a dancer (Anne's age), whose father is Italian and mother Belgian and who has lived nearly always in Paris. She speaks Italian, French and German fluently and she came to me to learn English. We became great friends and spent much of our time together. Her father, besides being a lawyer and a newspaper editor, is a dealer in antiques and their house is full (too full) of many precious things. Our life was very regular and, as Grandpa used to say, 'Our studies progressing well.' Signora Tamajo is a marvellous teacher and we were both terribly happy to learn with her. Our voices started blossoming out in an incredible way and we got more and more enthusiastic about her. I think we already described her to you in letters of 1940, a wiry, aristocratic little woman with terrific energy for insisting till her 'point gets home', but dangerous when in a bad temper. Lewis and I often went to Ostia with Adele and Philip and they often came and played cards with us at Pensione Nella. Even then we had got to the point of not speaking English outside the Pensione, but Lewis and Philip had a bad habit of forgetting this(!) and sometimes it became a little embarrassing in restaurants if we were heard speaking English. Though also in those days the majority of Italians were much more pro-Allie than pro-Axis. Very often in a bar the waiter would ask me what nationality I was. If I thought he was the right type I would tell him I was English whereupon he often gave me another drink, but if he was not the right type I would keep him guessing till I decided what nationality to answer to. I have been American (still at the beginning), French, Irish, Swedish, Danish, Hungarian, Swiss and Austrian – German never, because it was not popular. One day Lewis was reading a newspaper poster and a fierce-looking woman approached and as is the way in Italy broke at once into conversation. On seeing that Lewis spoke little Italian she asked him where he came from, and before Lewis had time to reply she said 'Are you German?' And Lewis, summing up her type, said 'Yes', whereupon she immediately broke into fluent German. Lewis hastened to say goodbye and escaped round the corner of the street. Another good friend of ours was (and is) Contessa Nora Balzani. We passed many interesting afternoons having tea at her house. Do you remember her well, Max? Tall, thin, rather beautiful, interesting and very intelligent. We like her very much. Well maybe there are many more things about that year which will come out later. In October 1940 (a few days after we had bought season tickets for a cycle of Verdi operas) we were called for the first time to the Central Police Station and interviewed by a rather unpleasant sandy-haired man (it is strange how unpleasant people often seem to be sandy-haired) who questioned us on why we were in Italy. When did we come, what we were doing, what money did we live on and didn't we understand we should probably be put in a Concentration Camp? Oh yes we said we understood that, but not believing that Italy would have come into the war we took the risk for the sake of music, and besides, we added, the American Embassy had told us by letter that the Italian Government would let us live in peace. He laughed and said the American Embassy did not count at all and this depended only on the Italian police who were likely to arrest us at any moment, but anyway we could go *for the moment*. We lived in fear for the next few weeks not wanting at any costs to be torn away from Tamajo, but we saw our operas through that season. Now the rations started in Italy, not very seriously until September 1941 when the chief things were cut down to a much smaller amount (then it seemed terrible but looking back now it would be wonderful to receive the amount we had then) – bread, macaroni, meat, butter, milk, cheese, eggs, etc. One day, in October 1941, a policeman arrived at Pensione Nella telling us to go to the police station with him. We dared not think what that meant. We hoped desperately that it was only for a regular questioning (which happened every now and then, but usually at Pensione Nella), or worse, that they had dis-covered that we were teaching English, but we realised the awful probability that they very likely wanted us to leave Rome. Having waited nervously for some time in the waiting room, we were ushered into the Office of the Political Police for foreigners, and told that we had to go to a Concentration Camp in Arezzo, a small country town near Florence. There of course there would be all the regulations of internment and they gave us eight days to pack up and go. In real desperation at the thought of leaving Tamajo I started crying and was only able to stammer out 'but we are going to be singers – we have voices – we have got to go on learning – we can't leave our teacher.' The Brigadier (about whom there is more later) was kind but apologetically said he was only carrying out orders from the Ministero dell'Interno (Ministry of Home Affairs) or perhaps Home Office (it would be in England) and we had to sign a piece of paper saying we would report to the police in Arezzo eight days later. We left the police station desperate but determined not to leave Rome. What could we do? We spoke to a lawyer friend of ours, and he helped us draft a petition to the Ministero dell'Interno, to the Head of the Police, explaining our whole situation and our reason for being in Italy, what we hoped to do in the future, how dangerous for the voice it was to change singing teachers in the middle of a course, and lastly begging for the generosity of the Italian Government in an exceptional case of two people who only wanted to study music. We sent this registered and waited patiently for the answer, getting one or two of our more influential acquaintances to recommend it in high quarters. The days passed and we prepared nothing to go away. On the eighth day we returned to the police station stating that we had applied to the Head of the Police and as yet the answer had not arrived. It had its effect and they agreed that the answer should be waited for. They postponed the date of departure on our papers for another week. And still no answer arrived. We wrote again begging for an urgent answer, and it was four times that the police changed our date of departure waiting for the answer which never arrived. Then they began to get annoyed with us and said we really must go in three days, and on no account and for nobody and for no reason would they change their mind – it was the last word. We began to lose hope and sadly think about how many suitcases we needed. What could we do? If only we could have a personal interview with the Head of the Police! Somehow we felt sure we could convince him, but we knew nobody who could introduce us to him and he seldom received anybody but the highest State Prefects. We seemed to be doomed. That evening Rosanna telephoned. It was the first time we had heard from her for quite a time as she had been away and consequently she knew nothing about our departure. When she heard she said 'Oh, my father knows the

Head of the Police well – they were at school together.'
You can imagine our joy! The father, at risk to himself
and his family, because everybody was frightened of doing
anything for anybody in Fascist wartime, especially for
two English people, wrote a letter to the Head of the
Police, and we, the day after, went to the Ministero
dell'Interno asking rather against hope for an interview
with the Head of the Police. We got it! And among all the
State leaders we were ushered first into his room. He was
extremely kind and said if it only depended on him he
would always leave us free, but unfortunately it depended
on the Military Authorities (which meant the Germans)
but anyway he would recommend the case to them. That
was marvellous but we explained that we had to be leaving
the next day! (And official red-tape in Italy takes a long
time.) Whereupon he ordered the Central Police Station to
give us a postponement of another week. Imagine their
wrath – especially the head who was rather a nasty little
man (he didn't have sandy hair this time) and had made up
his mind to get rid of us at any cost. Well, halfway through
the week Dr. Moretti, Rosanna's father, received a letter
from the Head of the Police saying that he had arranged
for the internment order on our behalf to be suspended
indefinitely. So even though we still had no official com-
munication, we knew we were saved. We were so happy at
the news and again we settled down to our programme of

study. But the extra eight days given us by the Police ended on Monday, and on Saturday two days before, I was having a singing lesson (as usual when anything happens, says Priscilla) when suddenly Lewis arrived all breathless to say that a policeman had been to Pensione Nella saying that our application had not been accepted and that we had to leave in any case and definitely at 6 o'clock on Monday morning. If we did not leave, action would be taken against us. We were puzzled and confused, not being able to understand what had happened. We raced to the Ministero dell'Interno to try and get in touch with the Head of the Police, but being Saturday it was closed and would be all day on Sunday, and we were supposed to leave early on Monday. We discussed it hectically with Dr. Moretti, and finally all came to the conclusion that this was a trick on the part of the police who were still angry at having had their authority questioned. We decided to risk this and go again to the Ministero on Monday morning, which we did and discovered that in fact the police *had* been acting against the orders of the Ministero, and in our presence the Ministero telephoned to them telling them just exactly to leave us alone, and they were forced to tear up our '*foglio di via*' (Internment Order) with very forced smiles. So that was settled, but of course we always had to be very careful and never provoke the attention of the Police who were authorised to intern people just on one single denouncement without bothering to go into the truth of it at all. So the best thing was just to let them forget you. — We hardly heard anything of Sigbert in those days, just occasional news through Signora Tamajo, and we were able to send only one other letter to him through an acquaintance whose brother-in-law was one of the Directors of the Concentration Camp and therefore it was given by hand. We knew that Sigbert was desperately trying to get back to Rome; we knew that he was giving concerts in the Concentration Camp; we knew naturally that he was very popular (because he always is wherever he goes, and that is not a biased opinion); and later in that year we knew something much more serious, and that was that the damp climate of Calabria and the draughts in the barracks where they lived had caused a chronic catarrh in his throat and his vocal chords were seriously affected. The doctor had ordered him to stop singing and to go twice a week to a nearby specialist, who told him that while he continued to live under the same conditions he would never be cured. So Sigbert made an application to the Ministero dell'Interno at Rome explaining his illness and the damaging effect it might always have for him and asking to be transferred in '*Confine libero*' (not a Concentration Camp but living almost free in a small village) in a healthier climate. After some months this was granted him and he was transferred to Picinisco, Province of Frosinone, in May 1942, where he lived in a beautiful house with friends in a very beautiful village – but more of this later. — Going back a little: our next difficulty was lack of food. We became very hungry and seldom had enough to eat. Pensione prices were going up and food was getting much less. We did not receive much subsidy from the Embassy and we could not pay the Pensione expenses so they gave us a smaller price but also gave us much less to eat. Sometimes we used to overhear the dealing out of the food in the kitchen. 'This is for the doctor, this is for Miss So-and-So, this is for the Captain and this (two small helpings) for the English couple.' We got so angry and weak and hungry and decided we must change house. When they discovered we wanted to go they got in the first word and said they wanted us to go because we weren't paying enough. On the last evening before we did leave we had a violent argument and told the Cavalier (proprietor of Pensione Nella) that after two-and-a-half years it wasn't the thing to do to turn us out at such short notice, especially as he knew all our history and difficulty of finding a room, but he said on the other hand he had been so decent to keep us there for such a long time at a low price thereby saving us this difficulty before. We changed in March 1942. It was very difficult for us to find a room: 1) because Rome was completely full of soldiers and refugees, etc 2) because we were English and not many people wanted us, not so much for personal resentment but for fear of compromising themselves; 3) because we should naturally bring our piano with us, and we were singing and playing all day; 4) because we could not afford to pay much and therefore hoped for a bargain; 5) because we wanted, if possible, to live near our friends, the Moretti family, who lived in the centre of Rome. Eventually we found a half-Italian, half-Scotch family who had lived most of their life in Scotland. There were the old father and mother, Mr and Mrs Abbate (he Italian, she Scotch), their two daughters, Irene and Ines, the husband of the latter and their two small children Milvio and Mauro. We realised they were a poor family but they seemed very kind and only too glad to have us plus piano, and for the first day everything went well. They were just all over us. (That is the only expression possible.) The food was good for the first day – but only the first. (A great advantage for us was that we were only two minutes from Rosanna who lived just in the street behind.) We spent six months in that place and how we did suffer. One trouble was that they were poor beyond every imagination earning hardly anything and being very lethargic about getting work, and we weren't much better off ourselves, but what we gave them, sufficient for our keep, had to be divided amongst the whole family – nine people instead of two, so that in the end we got hardly any food at all, and lessons being very low then, we could not buy extra food. Another reason was they seemed to believe our room was a kind of public sitting room and the whole family would pour in on us at any moment of the day – the children always dirty and wetting the bed – and they would chatter and chatter about nothing. Imagine poor Lewis trying to compose. Another trouble was (and I shudder to think of it) the room was full of beetles, fleas, mosquitoes, and – BED BUGS! Every night we would wake up being bitten all over and the smell of these last animals was so disgusting. We would switch on the light during the night and squash them with the end of my nail file, leaving bloody marks all over the sheets and pillows. We became so weak with not eating and not sleeping properly and the room was terribly hot and stuffy with the summer sun beating in all day that one day Lewis fainted in the street – poor darling, and I started a nervous break-down. I was unable to sing and every time I went to my lesson out of sheer weakness I began to cry instead – the very sight of a piano was enough to start me off; then when I went into shops I remained dumb not remembering what I had come in for or not being able to ask for it. We could only walk very small distances without collapsing for the rest of the day. I had a boy pupil who used to come for lessons every day, and as he paid me daily, this money we were able to use for eating in the evening, but unfortunately this boy usually preferred to go to the cinema with the money and in vain we spent the afternoon waiting for our food money and any amount of telephone conversations with the father did not alter this. You will say, but why did you stay so long in this awful place? Well, we were tied. You must remember that above all we did not want to call police attention on ourselves and when anybody changed room or house the police had to be immediately notified both by the present and future landlady and by the people themselves, but the main difficulty was in finding a room. We were continually searching, but in the meantime we tried to stamp out the bed bugs, which we succeeded in doing for seven weeks by employing an asphyxiating Gas Company to come and seal up the room and let in this very powerful gas. As for the food question: we got two spirit stoves and much against the will of the Abbate family, we kept on the room only and cooked for ourselves in our room. We got on better like that but of course by now food questions had become very difficult and we had not yet enough money to buy on the 'black market'. Rations had become so small that the amount they gave for one month was sufficient for about two days. (And that already in Summer 1942.) It was about this period that Dr. Moretti was arrested – one day in the street. As happens in this country he just didn't come home and nobody notified his family. But it wasn't difficult to imagine where he was, as he had been followed about in the street already for some time past, and he was known to be an anti-Fascist. The next day three policemen searched the Moretti house and amongst other things came across the letter the Head of the Police had written on our behalf, so he was then also accused of intriguing with English citizens. He was sent to prison for some time, then later to '*confine libero*' in a little village, then later put in a secret cell in the prison of Naples. — Well, towards the end of that summer our luck changed. All of a sudden people began realising the need of learning English again and very soon we had as many pupils as we wanted. It is rather difficult to describe this next period of our life as it was perhaps the most flourishing period of our life since we left England, in which we became quite famous and necessary to everyone at once. I seem to have spoken very little in this letter about our singing. This continued always regularly and steadily and in my case very successfully. Lewis, after two-and-a-half years, decided he was not getting on with Tamajo and yet did not want to go to another teacher, so he stopped learning with her and continued by himself. But for me she did wonders and my voice continually developed. I was studying mostly Italian music then – *Arie Antiche* and operas such as *Bohème*, *Traviata*, *La Sonnambula*, *Nozze di Figaro*, *Guglielmo Tell*, *Rigoletto*, *Butterfly*, etc. My voice being a mixture between a light and lyrical soprano (if you ever have the chance of talking to Cuthbert Smith please tell him these details. His address is 6 Queen Anne's Grove, W4 or at the Royal College of Music) and I developed a two-octave range, from middle C to top C and often taking D and E (these last I reached always in exercises without knowing it). Tamajo considered me as a kind of show pupil and was always showing me off in front of her friends and she said my throat had become completely Italian – which of course one always tries to attain, because our clipped English language of consonants tends to harden the throat making it less elastic to expansion. Lewis had begun by getting on well and had developed into a full bass-baritone but Tamajo has no patience with those who cannot learn to expand their throats and then she becomes devilish, loses her temper, crashes down on the piano and literally throws books around the room – but that is catching and sometimes during some of our heated arguments I did the same thing but with a hand mirror she had given me to sing into (in order to watch the position of the mouth). You certainly had to have a lot of patience with Tamajo (though she believed it was she who had to have it with us), who on the days when she is not sweet and docile is very temperamental and highly strung and starts shouting for nothing (often, of course, apologising the next moment). But I completely believed in her and my hopes were always higher as to my goal. — As I said before, our life changed. We found a lovely large room down the road (nearer still to Rosanna) and we moved there on September 1st 1942. A house belonging to Signora Venet and her sister; and our address became Via Babuino 51. We needed a large room because by that time we had enough things for a flat and we were completely self-contained in this room – it was a bedroom, music room, library (we had many English and Italian books) and kitchen all combined – for we still continued to cook on our two spirit stoves and having more money we were able to buy food on the black market – macaroni, rice, dried peas and beans etc, and sometimes butter when it could be found. Our lessons were numerous and well paid and all of a sudden we seemed to know all Rome and it became almost impossible to go out without meeting several people we knew. (Without being modest) I became well known as an English teacher and was always more in demand, receiving telephone calls every day from people begging me to teach them, as they had been told by so-and-so that I was the only teacher in Rome worth having etc. We made friends with lots of our pupils and were continually being invited here and there. One of our chief friends was and is Guido Cavallucci, a lawyer with wife and one child – then there was Principe B—, ex-Governor of Rome, who studied English with me with the express purpose of being able to understand the English Radio; then Esther and Sandro Laszlo, a charming young Hungarian couple; an Austrian family where I taught the child; Principe O— (the Governor of Rome) and family where Lewis taught the four children; Bruno Rovere, an Italian-American lawyer, and so many others, while we saw often Mrs D'Andrea (who was very kind to us, often inviting me to meals during our difficult 'starvation period'. She lives in the same house as Signora Tamajo) and Adele and Philip, and of course every day and every moment Rosanna, who used to drop in any moment she was passing – in fact she was like part of our family, almost. Our life was always filled in every moment – singing lessons four times a week (lessons of seldom less than one-and-a-half or often two hours or more). Signora Tamajo was always very generous with time as she had complete interest in my voice, and we would go on singing one thing after another without thinking of time. I was very happy in my singing lessons and every morning of a singing day I used to wake up excited at the thought of my lesson. Poor Tamajo did not get paid by us all during our difficult period with the Abbate family, but later we were able to pay back the debt. English lessons (they wanted me also to teach at the Berlitz school, but it was not worth my while, private lessons being much more paying); invitations – cooking etc (a lot of which Lewis did) – we lived in a complete wheel of movement, never having enough time to sleep, but we were happy. And clothes! I have always kept my dressmaker from four-and-a-half years ago as she is one of the best, and during that period I had many new clothes, always one thing after another, Rosanna and I buying and storing up the last woollen cloth and pure silk that was left in Rome, pouring in work on our dressmaker who dressed us both very well. (Priscilla and Anne what lovely feminine discussions we shall be able to have one day.) She made everything I wore – overcoats, winter and summer dresses, skirts, blouses, coats and skirts, house-coats, etc. And we bought many shoes, Angora jumpers, heavenly silk cami-knicks and had our hats made for us by a good milliner. Also Lewis had some new clothes, but not many as he preferred to buy music, gradually putting together a large amount of piano music – also duets, we spent all our free time playing piano duets together, that was a great joy: Beethoven symphonies, Mozart, Schubert, Brahms and some modern Italian music. By the way I have never mentioned our concerts. Every year we went regularly every week (often twice) to Symphony concerts – in the winter at 'Teatro Adriano' and in the summer out in the open air at 'Basilica di Massenzio'. They were beautiful and, combined with our regular operas, we got to know by heart much music.

It was on 17th December 1942 that Sigbert returned. It

was a rainy day, I remember, and as usual I had been out all day. I returned home in the evening at 9 o'clock. Our room was half in the dark and I knew Lewis would be lighting our wood fire (a stove which we had put in ourselves for the winter) in order to cook our evening meal. I opened the door, laden with parcels, and saw someone sitting on the sofa talking to Lewis. Sigbert! If it didn't sound romantic to say it I should say I was struck dumb, because that is the only way of expressing it. I stood at the door not knowing where I was and it was some seconds before I could speak. In that moment I knew I loved him as before. — That evening was the first of many that we spent happily all three together comparing notes and recounting details of the past two-and-a-half years we had not seen each other. Sigbert had finally succeeded in getting permission to come to Rome to see a throat specialist and undergo treatment. He even feared that his throat might not ever recover. He had changed — a little older-looking, much thinner and very worried-looking. He seemed at first to have lost his old spontaneous gaiety. He told us how he had been arrested at 7 o'clock on that morning of the 19th June, 1940. He had been out early and was at the market buying strawberries for us to bring to us in bed for a surprise. Someone he knew had called him and told him to go back to his house as he was wanted and there he found two policemen who told him to take a towel and a shirt and go with them. He was taken to the local police station, where they took away his tie and shoelaces and later in the day he was taken in a horrible black closed-in police car to the Rome prison – Regina Coeli – where he remained for three weeks. There he was in a cell with several others and of course the cell was full of bugs. He smoked all day, ate little and hardly slept at all, not knowing what would happen to them next. After three weeks they were all taken, hand-cuffed, to the station where they left by train for the Concentration Camp in Calabria. It was a long journey and during the night the hand-cuffs were so painful they could not sleep. On arrival they were greeted by the Director of the Camp, a very kind Napolitan, who ordered the hand-cuffs to be removed immediately saying that he would not see such treatment here, and adding that they were his guests and not his prisoners. But for this Director life in the Concentration Camp (Ferramonti it was called) might have been very unpleasant, but instead it developed into an intellectual and highly cultural self-contained colony of about two thousand people. There were barracks for single men and small houses for families; there was a school, a synagogue and a church where Sigbert ran the choir and taught the children singing. The camp was full of cultured people, including prominent musicians from all countries. Sigbert was famous for his concerts and also other things but later

Caricature of Sigbert conducting the choir at Ferramonti,
drawn by another inmate of the camp

we will tell you all the details of that camp for it was interesting. (Here I must keep to fact, otherwise the letter will be too heavy for the post, besides I want to get it off as soon as possible.) Well, Sigbert stayed in our house with us and he was in Rome that time for a month – passing Christmas and New Year of 1942/3 with us and Rosanna. Sigbert and I knew doubly strong again that we belonged to each other and life was beautiful. At the same time, strangely enough, also Lewis and Sigbert grew closer friends, and Lewis studied singing with Sigbert every day. Our evenings were very amusing. We always had a very late meal not starting to cook until everybody else had probably eaten (yes, Priscilla even we do that sometimes) because we were working late, and we used to laugh and joke and be silly. After dinner, about midnight, Lewis and Sigbert would send me to bed while they did the washing up, all of which took place in the same room. I would lie in bed and watch them, one washing and the other drying, in a tiny bowl of greasy cold water – poor darlings it was very cold. That month was very lovely. Sigbert and I were happy together scarcely thinking of how it was going to be possible to continue this happiness. We just knew we had to continue it. Sigbert had to go back to Picinisco. Lewis and I were very sad, and also his cure had hardly started, so we determined to try and get him back again. He made another application to the Ministero dell'Interno and we pulled strings here and twelve weeks later he came back to Rome. He found a room in the same street as us and stayed for three months. Of course we all lived entirely together all day, Lewis studied again, and they washed up again every evening while I was in bed, and it was lovely. (Here again details later.) Well, shortly before he had to leave, we were called to the police station and invited to leave Rome for any place, not military, at our own choice, where we could go on studying and doing what we pleased. We did not resist at all as we wanted to go to Picinisco with Sigbert. Also we were very tired and worn out after our hectic life in Rome. We had not been away since December

Maria and Sigbert in Rome in the summer of 1943

1939 (now it was June 1943) and studying was being hampered by this and Signora Tamajo was ill and could not teach any more (she gives herself nervous breakdowns every now and again) and we wanted to go on learning with Sigbert – but most of all we wanted to live with Sigbert. That was natural for me – I just could not live without him – but *Lewis* wanted to live with him: they became always greater friends. One day Sigbert said to me 'I can't live without you, but at the same time I don't want to live without Lewis. What does one do?' And almost the same day Lewis said to me 'You know Sigbert is my greatest friend. I grow always closer to him.' It was only Lewis and I who grew more and more apart from each other – in fact from December 1942 (when Sigbert returned) Lewis and I have remained completely apart in every sense. Well, Sigbert returned to Picinisco on July 1st to prepare everything. We would live in the same house as he and his friends, Dr. and Mrs Berent (he a judge of Danzig) and the two old parents of her, Mr and Mrs Knopff. So we should be seven in the house – and a piano – one of the few that existed in Picinisco because it was very tiny, there being only about 500 inhabitants. We imagined we should follow Sigbert very shortly, but it took ten and a half desperate weeks to get through all the red tape, and in the end they kind of decided that perhaps we were better left in Rome after all. Things were becoming muddled in Italy and they did not know what to do with us. So this time we had to fight to go to Picinisco, and we took no notice of a refusal we had from the Military Authorities. — During that period there was the 25th July. Lewis and I with Rosanna and Guido had been outside Rome on bicycles to eat at an old country farm and we arrived back in Rome at 10 o'clock. Everybody was clapping and shouting and the soldiers were cheering and we learned that Mussolini had been banished and Badoglio had taken over. The general relief and excitement was incredible. We spent all that night out watching the scenes in the streets. There were many fires especially a large one in the centre which we watched outside a Fascist headquarters where everything was being thrown out of the windows into the middle of the street – books, documents, flags, chairs, tables, cupboards and large photos of Mussolini. These all made a huge fire in the middle of the street, and amidst the general excitement and chaos Lewis calmly said 'It must be hot there.' Large photos of Mussolini were being brandished about with invitations to spit on them. I believe Lewis actually did – just for form's sake, you know. After this we imagined it would be very easy to get to Picinisco but it was more difficult still as military regulations were much stricter and nobody was allowed to travel, and by that time our trip to Picinisco was being regarded as our summer holidays. That was because we were so anxious to go and worried the police continually about us. 'Well, you've been trying to intern us all along, why don't you do it?' etc. — One day we achieved even this and we arrived at Picinisco on September 7th, being interned only for one day as the day after, of course, was the Armistice. (Now this next phase may be the longest to tell but perhaps the most interesting as being the most recent. Take a breath, dear; then we'll begin.) — Sigbert had not known the day of our arrival because the post was all out of order, and we left Rome immediately we heard the news ourselves deciding only to take the necessary amount of luggage with us and leave the rest in Rome. I left all my town dresses and clothes that I should not wear in the country with Rosanna – she had a flat of her own besides that of her parents. We packed up six large packing cases full of other things (books, music, saucepans, plates, old shoes, many handbags, gramophone, opera records, our famous earthenware kitchen stove with all its tubes which Sigbert called 'anti-aircraft-Leslie', and many other things) and these we left in a Hotel, the proprietor of which was a pupil of Lewis's by the name of Romano Gagliardi and he promised to take care of them. We left several other things with several other people, Lewis's dress suit, a portrait of Lewis painted by an American painter, a sculptured head of the sister of the painter done by a young girl pupil of mine aged 17 – very lovely work – and other things. After a very long journey (the trains were already partly out of action and we had to stop for bombardments on the way – by the way I haven't told you of the Rome bombardments in August 1943 but all details another time), we arrived at Picinisco at 6 o'clock on the 7th September 1943. Our arrival was very picturesque because nothing ever happens

Picinisco, Italy, 1943

in that tiny little village isolated from everything. The bus wound its way up in the mountains and we finally arrived in the village square crowded by colourfully dressed peasants because the arrival of the bus was a great event bringing with it the post and newspapers and an occasional holiday visitor. Immediately we saw Dr. and Mrs Berent and then Giuseppe and Jean D'Agostino, a half-Italian, half-Scotch couple whom we already knew and their two lovely small children – but Sigbert who had waited hopefully for that bus every single day just for once was not there. You can imagine his joy when he saw us – at first being unable to believe it, in fact he had almost given up hope. Sigbert had told us that Picinisco was beautiful but we had no idea it was *so* beautiful. A little white village high up in the mountains away from everywhere – clean and very picturesque, with a beautiful old tower in the centre and a lovely view all round. There were several newish houses in the village which were constructed by English people before the war for holidays and much in keeping with the old part of the village. We had the nicest house in the village (the owners of which are in England), large and white with a spacious balcony overlooking the valley of Atina (which you may have heard spoken about on the Radio lately). Every morning we had breakfast on this terrace – one of the most beautiful moments of the day, all the surrounding mountains appearing rather timid and hazy, and every evening Sigbert and I remained on the terrace when the others were in bed, and the mountains were black by that time and impressive – and that too was beautiful. As I said, the day after our arrival was the Armistice, and though everyone was mad with joy we somehow felt it had not yet finished. But the Allies were advancing and the general opinion was that in a few days they would have overtaken Picinisco and be well on their way to Rome. We felt rather safe there – high up in the mountains. We thought that a little place like that could have no military significance whatever, so at first we did not worry. For two weeks we lived in a lovely peace: Lewis started singing lessons immediately with Sigbert, but I wanted to rest a little first; we went for lovely walks in the mountains and slept a lot. Mrs. Berent was a good house manager and we all helped, dividing the jobs between us (Picinisco being very primitive), chopping wood, baking barley to make so-called coffee, drawing water out of the well in buckets (we shall hear more about this well later, so remember its existence), cooking and washing up and washing all the laundry under the village wells like the peasants, carting it there on a wheelbarrow; we made several acquaintances half of which were nearly English or had been brought up in England, as Picinisco had become almost a tiny English-Scotch-Italian colony before the war, and we were often invited out to tea, a beautiful habit which had not existed for us for years except on Sundays as a treat. We shall never forget one tea party with Giuseppe and Jean (who have a large Café in Edinburgh) when Jean made biscuits, scones and home-made doughnuts that were all squidgy and melted in your mouth. The memory of this helped us later in many unfortunate moments. One of the most beautiful things in our life in Picinisco were the evenings when Sigbert sang, accompanied by Mrs Berent. His voice was more beautiful then than I have ever heard it, he himself being in very good health from sun and air (his cure having been completed

The house in which Maria, Lewis and Sigbert lived in Picinisco

successfully during his stay in Rome) and being happy for our arrival. He sang wonderfully – night after night – going through piece after piece of his extensive repertoire, interpreting to perfection every type of music, and we were all happy listening to every word and note and watching his movements – for he sometimes walks about the room when he is singing or bursts out laughing when you least expect it. Afterwards we would go up on the balcony and eat grapes in the dark – dark except when there was a moon... Sigbert's musical library was his great pride – every piece being named and dated and separated into different files and appropriate drawers and all his operas and bound music arranged along shelves. Then we used to study languages, Sigbert starting learning English and Lewis and I German. But this beautiful life continued only two weeks. One morning we heard that a German soldier in Atina (nearby village) had said that the Germans were going to Picinisco to kill the Jewish internees, of which there were 14 in Picinisco. This was confirmed from other sources and it was decided to go into the mountains for a day or two to see what happened. This of course had to be kept secret. So the same evening eight of us including Lewis, Sigbert and I, set off in the dark with packs, and, led by a trusted boy in the village, went to a Grotto in the mountains where we stayed for five days – it wasn't bad then and it was summer so sleeping under the stars and living in the open space was nice. But after five days, as we had hoped, we found it was only a rumour spread by a drunk German. We came back to our lovely house but couldn't settle down as before; the Germans seemed to be nearer with too much of a tendency to close in on us, and the news was not good: re-instatement of Fascism and Germanism in Rome, liberation of Mussolini, hold up of Allies on South front etc. Then one day a German car arrived in Picinisco and ten minutes later the local police came to our house to see if we had a radio as they always heard music when they passed – oh they knew it was Sigbert singing and Lewis playing but they had to make sure. Then another day the Germans arrived and took away all the olive oil in the village, another day all the flour, then the pigs and chickens; and people began hiding what they had left. We decided that the Germans knew too much about Picinisco and we prepared for an emergency. We took all our best clothes – new winter overcoats never worn, leather shoes, all our pullovers, underclothes etc. and limiting ourselves to one or two suitcases each we hid them in the well in the garden – that is, not as far down as the water but in a concrete corridor which could not be seen from the top and had to be reached by a step ladder like this:

opening to well

concrete passage

our suitcases

water

At the same time we packed one small bag or basket each and prepared a few blankets and left everything always ready for an emergency. We were always able to hear a motorcar long before it arrived at Picinisco and we could see it in the distance gradually climbing the mountains. But we were rather nervous and sometimes imagined things we didn't really hear. When a German car or lorry did arrive we went for a walk in the woods and did not come back until we knew it had gone, sometimes remaining out three or four hours just around lunchtime which was very tiresome of them. One day – it was 10th October 1943 – Dr. Berent, Lewis and Sigbert had gone out early to transport some things for safety measures; Mrs Berent and I had arranged breakfast on the terrace. It was 8 o'clock, and suddenly we heard the noise of engines. Looking down into the distance we saw six large German lorries arriving full of soldiers. There was no doubt. We picked up our baskets, the men arrived back that moment and we five (leaving Mrs Berent's mother in charge of someone in the village – she is old – the father in the meantime had died) walked out of the back door as the Germans passed the front door. We soon learnt that they had come to occupy the village and instate a German Command, and we also learned that they had immediately taken over our house, being one of the nicest, and several others. So there we were in the woods without house or possessions. But we imagined that the Germans would not stay long as of course we thought the front was advancing. We spent the first two nights in a little stone hut but then the proprietor came wanting to use it for hiding sheets and things; the next two nights we spent in an open straw shack and it began to rain. On the second night there we were woken at midnight [to learn] that Italy and Germany were fully at war, and all the young men from Picinisco had gone away and the Germans were beginning to look for people. So, of course, we had to find a better hiding place, and against our will we decided to go back to our first Grotto (by the way, the word Grotto means 'cave' – and not the blue kind of floaty thing that we mean by the word. This was just a kind of shallow hollow in the rocks high up in the mountains) – against our will because it was a very cold place being completely open, just a mass of rocks, and the sun never reached it so that it was dark and chilly. We left the same night in the rain and having tramped for several hours in the woods amongst brambles and ditches, and having lost our way and been obliged to wait until it was light, we arrived in the early morning at our Grotto. We

Picinisco and surrounding mountains, 1943

were rather depressed and it looked so bleak and everything was wet and slippery and grey, but we thought it
would all be over soon. We thought – 'The English will
soon be here, so we can resist here for about ten days if
necessary.' But ten days seemed an exaggeration and we
thought how awful. Looking back now it was as well we
did not know that we would stay there for three months.
And that is what happened – we stayed there until the last
day of December, including Christmas and everything. We
lived in two adjoining Grottos – Dr. and Mrs Berent in one
and Lewis and Sigbert and I in the other. Ours was the
smallest and we had no room to stretch ourselves at all.
We slept all huddled up against each other, half balanced
on the rocks. For all those months the three men did not go
out at all as the Germans were all round us – except Lewis
who used to descend a precipice every night in the dark
with bottles tied on to his back to get water. Mrs Berent
and I used to get the food. I would go back to Picinisco
using the woods of acquaintances of ours and keeping
myself hidden; and Mrs Berent would go to the neigh-
bouring village called Fonteduno. In all those weeks we ate
or drank nothing hot, not being able to make a fire as the
smoke would be seen; we lived on bread and cheese, apples
and bacon fat and water. In the beginning the weather was
fine and we used to laugh and joke and study English and
German and play cards; Lewis was marvellous and filled

many copybooks with short stories. Sigbert and I used to write down all our dreams, which also made quite an interesting book. Until the end of November Sigbert and I used to sleep up above the Grotto under the stars, making our beds of sticks and moss and entering the Grotto in the morning at the first crack of light so as not to be seen. Sometimes it was very beautiful up there when there was a moon and the mountains and trees looked so lovely. — But in the beginning of December it became too cold so we had to join Lewis in the little Grotto, which did not please him very much as he could no longer lie flat. But we managed somehow. Lewis made himself an ingenious kind of bed which jutted out over the edge (because any false step on our part and we were down) and he dug me a hole to sit in as I became quite sore from sitting on rocks – but the rocks never disappeared. The trouble was when it rained – within a few minutes everything was wet and the occasional drops from rock edges turned into rivulets – later it also snowed and then the rocks became almost too slippery to move about on. Then one day we were told by someone in Picinisco that the German Commandant, the evening before having been a bit drunk, said 'Ah, we know there's an English girl who comes into Picinisco every day to get food for other people who are hiding. But we're on her track and we'll get them all!' So after that I hardly ever went to Picinisco. Then there was the time when the Germans put up notices on the walls saying everybody was to return to their own homes within five days, after which anybody found in the caves or in the woods would be shot on sight (man or woman the same). Everybody returned except us five. We figured it this way – if we returned we should be shot anyhow (*perhaps* Lewis and I might have escaped with Concentration Camp but for the other three it was certainly the end) and there was always hope of not being shot if we continued to hide (and anyway we had no house to return to). So Mrs Berent and I went to Fonteduno to lay in enough food for ten days. We brought all the food we could find and came staggering back over the mountains with sacks, each carrying about 18 kilos. We tried to get back without being seen but we passed a group of German officers who eyed our sacks and observed that we were probably coming down from the mountains, 'Oh yes,' we said, 'we're on our way back.' Only the surrounding peasants knew we weren't really peasants and started asking us where we came from – it was so inquisitive of them, and one old lady nudged her husband and said in an obviously loud voice, 'Ssh, don't you see they don't want to tell' – oh, poor dear, and she tried to be so tactful. But it was all right and we got gradually back to the Grotto – but it took us a long time, everything was so heavy and then it got dark and then my shoes completely gave way and I had to walk bare-footed and there were lots of brambles and stones and everything was wet and slippery. But we got back and none of us went out of the Grotto again for ten days. — During that time, as we later learnt, the Germans made a thorough search, sending large patrols of soldiers in every direction capturing many English prisoners of war who were also hidden, and making extensive enquiries in Picinisco as to the whereabouts of the Jewish internees. Fortunately nobody knew where we were as we had told everybody we were in quite the opposite direction. Then one day I crept back to Picinisco, but our acquaintances (Carlo Alberto Mancini and his wife Virginia and family) were frightened to see me by that time as there was a death penalty for those who gave hospitality or hid Jews or English, but Carlo Alberto told me that the day before a German officer had said to him 'Do you know a man by the name of Sigbert Steinfeld? He is quite a well-known artist from Berlin – a singer and film actor. Well, he escaped from Berlin and as he is a great spy we must catch him at all costs. He lived in that house over there – don't you know him?' Apparently the Commandant walked furiously up and down the village square every morning, beating his stick on his boots and shouting out aggressively, 'Where is this Steinfeld? I want Steinfeld. I want Steinfeld.' Then one day, in our house, an officer talking to a charwoman threw a bunch of Sigbert's ties to her and said 'Here, take these along to your husband — they belong to a man we've got to find anyway. Where is he?' The charwoman, instead of taking the ties, threw up her hands in mock horror and said, 'For goodness sake! I wouldn't touch these for anything. This man died two months ago from T.B.!' Whereupon the officers became a bit nervous and carted Sigbert's two large suitcases, containing many precious documents (affidavits, letters of personal recommendation for America, singing contracts in Brazil and New York, letters from the New York Bank, singing reviews and write-ups both from Germany and Italy, certificates from various professors; Conservatorium diplomas, not to mention all personal letters and photographs and stage photos) into the garden and set fire to them. We knew the Germans had broken all the doors and windows of our house, we knew they had stolen everything that was left in the house, but it was a very sad day when we heard they had taken away all the music. Ours and Mrs Berent's was comparatively small, but Sigbert's — think of all that large, well-chosen and beloved music library of his — they stole every piece. So much of it can never be replaced, being either music out of print or original music which had belonged to his father. — We had made arrangements with the Podesta of Picinisco (that means a kind of village mayor) that when the Germans had gone he would put up a white flag on the tower of Picinisco to let us know, and

Dr. Berent (who you must know is rather a ridiculous and comical man, being of an extremely hard and rigid Prussian type and therefore funny without knowing it) would emerge out of the Grotto every morning at dawn with his famous binoculars (left over from the last war, you know) and spend the next quarter of an hour looking for the flag – every morning the same routine, and every morning, poor man, he would come crawling back into the Grotto and, balancing on a rock with an expressionless face, he would issue in a stentorious voice the same sentence: '*Nessuna bandiera*' (which means 'No flag'). We just shrieked with laughter especially when Sigbert stood behind him and mimicked every movement he made. Those binoculars came out on every possible occasion: for every dog that climbed the opposite mountain; for every stone that rolled; for every leaf that stirred; almost for every flea that attacked us. He was rather a pathetic man really – because he is unable to really laugh; so maybe he suffered in the Grotto more than any of us. — But Lewis suffered very much in the Grotto because he guessed everything between Sigbert and I, as I was unable to hide my feelings – but more than that because when Lewis and I were alone I was unable to pretend what I didn't feel. And yet it was still the wrong moment for Sigbert and I to speak to Lewis – in such desperate circumstances – so by necessity we continued to deny it, even on the occasion when Lewis even offered me divorce if I really felt that I had found the man I wanted to live with all my life. The situation was very delicate as you can imagine, all three of us all day and all night living in the smallest space possible for three months. But as I have said before, Lewis and Sigbert were the greatest friends. We could think of no solution that could avoid hurting Lewis. Sometimes Sigbert would say he would just disappear – two men can't live with one girl so the last-comer must go, and if this last-comer could not live without the girl it would be better just not to live. But it was too late; my mind was made up already from December 1942 and none of these solutions could bring happiness to any one of us three. For some time I had some idealistic notions that we three could always live together – but somehow with Sigbert and Lewis changing places – because I knew I wanted to be Sigbert's wife, but I still couldn't conceive leaving Lewis. You see I have had a terrible battle between my loyalty to Lewis and remembrance of all our past joy and my love for Sigbert, but the latter was the strongest, even stronger than my life with Lewis had been and the terrible thought of breaking Lewis's life. Well, even Lewis thought we three could continue to live together – but of course keeping intact the single unit between Lewis and I and treating Sigbert as the best friend of that unit. We made plans about coming back to London and living all three in a flat, and we would continue to study singing with Sigbert. But it was in Picinisco I began to see the impossibility of this because Lewis and Sigbert started all of a sudden being not such good friends – especially in the Grotto. You see they are both completely opposite types and this came out even more so in the Grotto, where Lewis always remained calm and philosophical and Sigbert being very highly strung became nervy. On the days when I went to Picinisco (being away from the Grotto four or five hours at a time) Sigbert would not be able to rest one moment in peace or think of anything else till I got back. He would pace up and down looking out of the top of the Grotto in the direction from which I would come, and he wouldn't eat anything, and if I was any later than the time I was supposed to arrive he was already sure that the Germans had caught me and would return immediately to give himself up to them. He could not understand how Lewis could sit calmly and write stories, but Lewis said, 'I know Mary.' One day, it was a Sunday afternoon in November, Sigbert was crossing from our Grotto to the Berents' when he heard a shout and, looking round, on the opposite bank not very far away, he saw a German soldier looking up in our direction. I, who knew nothing, had followed Sigbert and I saw him and Dr. and Mrs Berent crouching behind the rocks in the Grotto. Of course, the passage between the two Grottos was visible from opposite, and we felt sure the German must have seen us. We heard the latter giving directions to another soldier who seemed to be just below our Grotto: 'Goodfeld, higher up, and more to the left – further up still.' We thought it was the end for us and I could hear Sigbert's heart beating so loudly. (Of course, the binoculars were already out.) We waited and watched and they went on giving directions. Then suddenly we heard a terrific explosion and Lewis's books fell from his hand. Were they trying to blow us up, or what was happening? After a few moments, another explosion, and later another. It was a horrible, ear-cracking noise and so near. But nothing else happened and at last we succeeded in persuading ourselves that perhaps they really hadn't seen us. Then we had the happy idea that they were blowing up bridges as a last action before leaving Picinisco – oh, what a heavenly thought! But we learnt only the next day that the Germans had had a taste for fish and by means of dynamite had been harvesting trout from the river! You see, we really did imagine the Allies were advancing because we were only eight miles from the fighting line and it was as noisy as if we were right at the front – cannon-shells bursting all round us and bombardments and anti-aircraft and rifle shots which seemed so near. We used to hear the departure and the arrival of the cannon shots and that long shrill whistle as they passed over our heads. I remember one day when I went to Picinisco I had to throw myself down on the ground every few moments while I saw the shrapnel bursting on the tree trunks. And one morning at dawn we saw several red lights accompanied by rifle shots and Dr. Berent (who was in the last war and so knows everything about war proceedings) was convinced they were the first English patrols, and nothing any of us could say would convince him to the contrary. After that everything we saw became for us 'The first English patrols'. It was only for this that we resisted out there for all that time. We were innocent enough to believe that one day the Germans would just go away, the English would arrive and we would come out on the right side, so we went on living, becoming more and more like beasts, washing ourselves only once a week and then with only a saucerful of water, and never changing our clothes (we had no others) which by that time were falling off us from dirt and wear and having only one blanket each. It was terribly cold – the mountains were high – and Sigbert and I used to spend all night and most of the day completely under the cover, head and all. Lewis would bravely continue writing with his head and his hands all wrapped up in his blanket – for we had no stockings or gloves or anything like that and Sigbert and Lewis had no coats (I had my old teddy-bear). We even read, wrote and did mending under this blanket. Oh! The mending! Right from the first everything was torn because wherever we moved there were jagged rocks and Sigbert was continually without elbows and with large holes in the back of his trousers, while every part of Lewis's trousers and mackintosh was torn from his perilous descent for water – and their socks just weren't socks! Mrs Berent and I cut pieces from inside linings and things and patched up as best we could. Mrs Berent is good at anything housewifely and sometimes she would trail all across those mountains – a three-hour journey – in the pouring rain to get food. It was awful if one of us came back wet because it meant just sitting in wet clothes all through the night as we had nothing to change into. Then we had a great trouble – we ran out of shoes! The shoes we had come out in just didn't stand up to anything. The three men all had broken shoes; but except for Lewis, they did not have to move about much. But Mrs Berent and I had great difficulty till one day someone in Picinisco presented me with a brand new pair of mountain boots, so after that we shared those, but it meant that we could never go out at the same time. Can you imagine the nights in the Grotto? It was already dark there at half past four so we had to have our last meal at four o'clock (no lights, no fires) and after that it was pitch dark till seven o'clock the next morning. We were actually asleep by about 7.30 in the evening (I should say I was, being the only one who slept fairly well, though only sitting up against rocks – you see I take after Max in this) and slept till about midnight, when I would wake up for certain physical necessities, dear, and then I would sleep again till about 6 o'clock. Of course any time one of us woke, all three of us woke (it really *was* a case of when Pa turns they all turn) and if any one of us pulled a blanket, the other two hadn't got any. And if every inch of the blanket was not closed all round the neck, etc, the wind was icy. But the strange thing was our health was marvellous (except that Sigbert had bad toothache sometimes which was terrible without enough Aspirin and it being so cold). We never once had any colds and we became as strong as peasants in spite of not eating enough. Well I could go on describing our Grotto life for ages in all its details and looking back on that life now it seems unreal and one can even laugh about it – we can laugh not because it was funny but because now we are safe and then we lived in continual fear of ending our lives within the next 24 hours – in fact sometimes there seemed to be no hope left at all and no future beyond the grey rocks around us which did not even protect us from the rain. On Christmas day the Podesta of the village sent us some meat and a bottle of red wine, and three small shepherd boys (who had discovered us once by mistake, much to our subsequent anxiety and whom we had to bribe to keep quiet by promising them 100 lire each if they brought us the good news of the arrival of the

Allies. Once they did bring us some news: they said Russia had made peace with the Germans and was now fighting against the Allies – and for that I think they expected their hundred lire) brought us some mutton cooked by themselves. But towards the end we really did get desperate – there seemed no way out and the circle seemed to be enclosing closer and closer around us. What *could* we do? How much longer could we go on living like that? Would it be possible to bear January and February out there in the icy cold? Or did one die when it became too cold? Then something decided us. One day we heard that Fonteduno (the little village that fed us) had been suddenly evacuated. Without any warning the German lorries had taken the peasants away from their homes within an hour, and they threatened to do the same thing to Picinisco. So we should have to move. We couldn't stay without any food in German-occupied territory evacuated from all Italians. After much discussion the two Berents decided they would risk going back to Picinisco to join her mother who had remained there all the time, and we three decided we would try and reach Rome, though we were rather without hope at this attempt as we had no documents and we had heard all sorts of stories about there being a cordon of soldiers all round Rome and no one could pass without Roman documents. But we thought if only we could reach Rome, Rosanna would hide us somehow.

Mrs Berent had not been gone many hours before she came hurrying back and said, 'Oh everything's different in Picinisco. The German Command has gone and there is an Austrian Command instead, but they are all soldiers who care for nothing else but drinking and laughing and they take no notice of anybody. Do come back too and we can all live for the moment in the same house as my mother and Mrs Salstein (another Jewish internee with two small children). So that night in the dark we went to Picinisco and for the next ten days Lewis, Sigbert and I lived in a tiny room in a cottage without going out or being seen by anybody. The cottage was dirty and primitive but we thought it was lovely. It seemed impossible to be within four walls again and to be able to drink hot soup and to lie flat on a hard floor, even without anything underneath, was absolute heaven. During the ten days we spent there we made friends with the interpreter to the German Command, through a rather strange incident: one day, several weeks before, the few Jewish women who were left in Picinisco had been called up by the Commandant who had pinned a large yellow star on each one – just to point out to everyone that they were Jews, you know – and the day after, Mrs Knopff (Mrs Berent's mother) was standing in a queue for a few grams of salt when the interpreter came up to her and said, 'You are a Jew, you must go to the end of the queue, and if there is any salt left after you

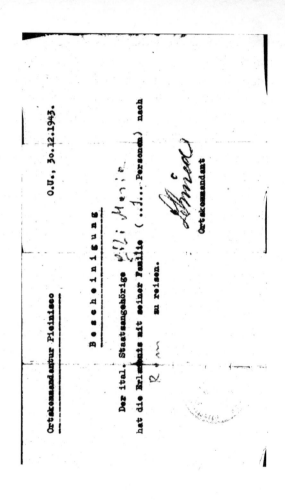

The false German document produced for Maria
by the interpreter

can have it.' She thought she had seen him somewhere before, and she talked about it later to Mrs Salstein who also thought she had seen his wife before. Then they remembered – they were all together in the Calabrian Concentration Camp! So they told the wife they knew who they were and both she and her husband, the famous interpreter, begged them not to tell anybody – that they were doing this work with a double purpose and with the scope of helping English prisoners, and that the Germans thought they were Italian. The interpreter was very kind to us. He came to visit us sometimes by dark and he said to us three: 'Nobody knows you are here – stay in and don't let yourselves be seen – if there is any danger I will come and tell you.' (He brought us some bread and cigarettes). Then one night he came and said 'You must leave at once – tomorrow the lorries are coming to evacuate Picinisco and you will be taken all in a mass to Ferentino where you will all be divided out and asked for documents. You must leave before it is light.' He wrote for each one of us a document in German with the German stamp saying we were Italian civilians who wanted to reach our families in Rome, but he said to Lewis, 'You can't possibly pass as Italian. Not only that you don't speak Italian well but in every movement you can see you are English. It would be dangerous for you to go without your passport.' (I had already hidden mine in the Grotto, with photographs, anything that was written in English and everything we had written while in the Grotto, and we had cut off all English and German labels, such as on shirts, ties etc.) So Lewis said he wanted to go alone so as not to compromise anyone else, and he said to Sigbert and I: 'You two go together – you can pass as Italians – as husband and wife if you like – and try and get into Rome. When in Rome find John (an Austrian friend of ours who had permission to use his car where he liked) and get him to come out of Rome to fetch me. Meanwhile, I will get as near as Rome as possible.' We spent that night packing up and deciding what to do, and before it was light we set off in three groups – the Berents, Sigbert and I, and Lewis alone, thinking we should all meet again in a few days' time. It was very cold and we had very little on (it had been impossible to rescue our clothes from the well as the garden was full of Germans). We were dirty and torn and looked like tramps. Sigbert was carrying a sack over his shoulder and I had two small bags. We began to walk and walk, rather nervously at first but we soon realised that the soldiers we met couldn't tell who we were – we felt so self-conscious and it was strange to come out and see people again. Sigbert who had not walked for three months was very wobbly at first and very stiff later. Every now and again we ate bread and cheese by the side of the road and then we walked, 10, 20, 25, 30 kilometres. Then we travelled in a

German lorry; then another! Yes, Sigbert started talking with the soldiers pretending he only knew a bit of German (playing with fire, dear, playing with fire) and they gave us lifts. If only they had known who they had got. The first night we spent at Sora which was half in ruins from bombs, the next day we took two more German lorries and arrived nearly at dark near Palestrina. There we stopped an old peasant and begged him to take us to his house for the night (just to give us two chairs to sit on during curfew hours). 'Oh no,' he said, 'my house is little and poor, but I will take you to the Hotel at Palestrina – just the place, nice Hotel – now it's full of Germans.' We looked at each other thinking *just* the place for us, and we begged the man to let us go to his house as we were too dirty, etc, to go to a Hotel. Finally, he agreed, and he even gave us a camp bed for the night, but, poor man, he had the fright of his life – so did we – for at one o'clock in the night the door was broken open and two Germans with a large flash-light broke into the room. Sigbert quick-ly directed them to the landlord's room (nothing to do with us, sort of thing) and having made a bit of a noise they went out again – probably only drunk and not after Sigbert and Mary after all. The next day we set off at 5a.m. and walked and walked but that day we had no suc-cess with German lorries. At mid-day, thoroughly exhaust-ed and hungry, we arrived at Colonna (a little village not far from Rome) where we exchanged a shirt of Sigbert's for a large loaf of bread. We couldn't walk any further so we decided to risk taking the little electric train and hoped that nobody would stop us on our arrival at the station, but so as not to look suspicious we deposited the sack with the station-master thinking that in a few days time Rosanna and I would be able to come out with suitcases and collect it (but alas we never saw that sack again). So after a journey of three days instead of normally two and a half hours we arrived at Rome on Sunday 9th January of this year. Our intention was of course to go to Rosanna who would hide us and also give me all my clothes. We got out at the station trying to feel very casual as if we did this sort of thing every day. We went straight to a telephone box – it was 5 o'clock, two hours before curfew. I telephoned Rosanna but was answered by a strange voice who told me Rosanna was away from Rome, also her mother. The father I did not ask for as I knew he would be in hiding somewhere after his previous experiences (by the way on the 25th July 1943 naturally he had at once been let out of prison). I thought it rather strange that Rosanna should be away during the opera season (because she is in the opera ballet). Then I telephoned John – no answer and I later learned that he had been transferred to Zagreb. Telephoned Guido – he was out. Oh dear, what should we do? We didn't want to be caught on the first night. Then

Sigbert telephoned some friends of his – a very charming German journalist (anti-Nazi, of course) with a Jewish wife (Mr and Mrs Schott). He was out and she answered, and not wanting to be explicit and give names on the telephone Sigbert just said we would come and see her. Which we did – imagine the following picture: we arrived at this beautiful, modern and choicely decorated flat, and the door was opened by Mrs Schott herself accompanied by a friend – two tall, elegantly-dressed women smoking with long cigarette-holders and in a perfect setting of comfort. We, Sigbert and I, stood on the threshold dirty and torn – Sigbert with the old mackintosh we had slept on for three months, torn trousers, muddy boots, an old battered hat given to him by the Podesta's brother for the purpose of the journey, and the beginnings of a moustache which had to be grown to hide his features. I – in the old teddy bear coat which was filthy and torn, muddy boots, a red handkerchief on my head in the peasant style and this wretched bag in my hand – you must remember our hands and faces and legs were begrimed. We stood there and she put her hand to her mouth in horror and clutched her friend. 'Oh, who are you? – who are you?' she said. Sigbert removed his hat and came nearer 'I am Steinfeld' – 'Oh no, it's not true – it's not possible – it couldn't be.' Sigbert insisted that it was possible and slowly a sign of recognition spread over her face, whereupon he explained what had happened, that we were stranded and needed only two chairs to pass the night on – we would go away immediately in the morning. 'Oh I couldn't do that,' she said (there was death penalty for those who hid English or Jews). 'You see I have my small daughter here and she might talk at school, and then there's the porter (all porters, by the way, were paid Fascist spies and had to be informed of anybody who visited a member in the building), he will have seen you come up – it's too dangerous, and yet if I don't help in this moment I shall have it on my conscience all m life – oh I don't know what to do.' Then she looked me up and down and said rather disdainfully: 'Besides I don't know this woman.' 'Oh,' said Sigbert, 'don't worry, your husband does.' At that moment the bell rang – we were still standing in the hall – and in a frightened whisper she said, 'Oh these are some German friends of mine – come here quickly,' and she shoved us into the lavatory where we remained for the next half hour. Then, fortunately for us, we heard the husband return and the friends went away – it was nearly seven o'clock and they couldn't turn us out. The husband fetched us from the lavatory and was very jovial and kind – said we could stay that night if we were very careful and went away in the morning separately. So that was our first evening of civilisation; a nice hot meal and a comfortable bed and pleasant surroundings. The next morning we went straight to Rosanna's house and were greeted by the mother in tears who said that Rosanna had been in the German prison for already two months (because she had helped Badoglian groups and been discovered), the father was hidden somewhere she didn't know where and she had been hidden in a sanatorium for two months and had only just returned home. After Rosanna had been arrested the house had been left in the hands of a Russian prince and the Germans had ransacked and stolen a large amount of things, including nearly all my clothes – a lovely grey winter overcoat, Angora jumpers, skirts, winter dresses; materials and other things, so in the middle of winter I found the only clothes I had left were a few summer and spring dresses and a white mackintosh. Then we went to Guido who immediately gave us some money and said we could sleep in his offices till he could find a hiding place for us. We spent the next two nights in these newspaper offices, and then Guido, with a lot of skill, put us in a Convent (which was only meant for girls) saying we were Italians from the South, our house had been bombed and we had lost all our documents – that soon we should be having others but in the meantime to look after us. We stayed there for ten days and Guido paid all the expenses for us. During that time we set about trying to get false Italian documents and ration cards, which we finally did (and in fact during the next few weeks we got hold of a varied selection of identity cards from Naples, Salerno, Catania, Rome and Angri; some of which we filled in with false names and others we left blank in case of emergency. Every day we were waiting for Lewis to arrive, imagining he would get into Rome as easily as we had despite the fact of John's absence. The Berents had already arrived and were living in a room which they had found with the help of Mrs Moretti. But one day Romano Gagliardi, the proprietor of the Hotel where Lewis and I had left all those packing cases before leaving Rome, telephoned me to meet him urgently, which I did, and he said that the German Police had come to the Hotel asking for the luggage of 'Leslie' [Lewis's surname] and that they were coming back again. They did come back the next day – BRINGING LEWIS WITH THEM. That was the first thing we heard that they had caught Lewis. In Lewis's presence they had turned everything out looking through everything – they took very little away except photos of me, but they said they were coming back for the rest. (But the carpenter who opened the cases later stole many things – gramophone, records, jumpers, handbags, books and other precious personal things). Then we learnt from the Swiss Legation that Lewis had been put in Regina Coeli (Rome Prison) in the German branch. The Swiss Legation made an appeal to the German authorities explaining Lewis's position and asking them to put him back under

Sigbert and Maria, on their return
from the grotto, February 1944

their protection as before. No answer was received and we knew no details at all. We tried by secret sources to get him out even though we had no money (such things are sometimes achieved by money here) but all was useless and we were not able to get in touch with him at all except to see that the Swiss took him some Red Cross parcels and something warm to put on (in Regina Coeli one eats nothing but bread and a watery soup in the middle of the day). — In the meantime I went again to the Morettis' house and Mrs Moretti practically pushed me out of the door, saying: 'For goodness sake Mary, don't come here. The Germans are looking for you everywhere – they came here yesterday evening and this morning with your photographs. I told them I had only seen you once several weeks ago, that you hadn't been here since and I didn't know where you were. But they didn't believe me and said that they knew you were hiding either here or in Rosanna's flat. So you must disappear and not be seen round here.' That was serious because if they caught me it would inevitably be the end of both Sigbert and I – and if we were traced back to the Convent it would be bad for Guido who was already in political difficulties. So we left the Convent the same day not knowing where we were going (fortunately we had little luggage because we had nothing – it was dangerous to be seen with suitcases). We went to visit some friends in the Vatican City – a Swiss couple, Peppino and Elsa Imesch, he being the Sergeant of the Swiss guards, and there to our great luck (we have always had luck in critical moments – Sigbert says I have a lucky star) we found the maid of Sigbert's landlady of before the war, Domenica by name, who knew us both. She said at once, 'Oh, you can come to my house, nobody will find you there and you can stay as long as you like.' So we went with her, her house being on the outskirts of Rome right in the bombardment areas, and her house was about the only one left standing in the street, everything all round being a mass of bricks. In those days there were aerial alarms every few moments. We stayed there for ten days but the Germans were still looking for me and it was necessary to find a place where I could remain indoors as we had to leave Domenica's house every morning till the evening owing to the bombardments. So for the next three weeks I stayed with our Hungarian friends, Esther and Sandro Laszlo; and Sigbert continued to stay with Domenica, every now and then spending nights at two other houses to avoid always being seen returning to the same place. I did not go out at all while I was with Esther and Sandro and for them it was very dangerous – if the porter or their maid got to know they could have been shot immediately, so I was always having to hide, and the flat is very small – I slept on the floor of their bedroom which during the day was transformed into the sitting-room. There were French windows to the room and we had arranged a system whereby I should climb across the balcony into the balcony of the next house if the bell rang during the night. Esther and Sandro are very charming and naturally and spontaneously kind and generous. Esther immediately lent me underclothes and a nightdress, a friend of hers gave me a skirt, Guido's wife gave me a jacket, and another woman we know gave me a cardigan and a pair of gloves. Then we had fresh worries. The Germans started making raids in the streets: they would close whole streets with soldiers and arrest every man in the street and take them on lorries to the North of Italy for defence work. They would do this at every moment and in any place. Suddenly they would stop and surround a bus or tram and take out all the men, or surround cigarette queues or enter cinemas, and of course the men started staying indoors. I was very frightened for Sigbert – for this and also because they were searching everywhere for the Jews and stopping men in the streets whom they thought looked Jewish. He had several very near shaves when streets were blocked – it would have been awful if he had been discovered with false documents too. So we decided that perhaps by now the Germans were not looking for me so much – we would find a room together and perhaps Sigbert would be able to stay indoors more, and anyway we had been separated for three weeks and could not bear it any more. We found a room in the same house as the Berents in the centre of Rome – Via Veneto. We had intended to take this room only for a few nights until we found something else; for one reason because the Berents were there, and we thought four people in the same conditions was a bit too dangerous, and another reason because it is the street of all the big Hotels which were all full of Germans and Supreme Commands and German Police Headquarters and all those sort of things. The family consists of Mr and Mrs Chierichetti and their son Mario – all very kind. We told them nothing about us except that we were Costantino (Tino for short) and Maria Santarelli, that we were refugees from the Cassino direction, our house had been bombed, we had lost all our possessions including our identity documents, and we begged them not to tell the Police we were here as they were sending all Italian refugees North of Rome and we did not wish to leave Rome. They believed everything we told them and said they would not tell the police (we had to tip the porter heavily every month). This was during this last February. So Tino and Maria became real Italians, forgetting they had ever been called anything else but Santarelli. We lived through a period of continual uncertainty and anxiety – in a tiny little room without clothes money or possessions but worst of all being frightened all the time of being arrested. When either of us was only a few minutes late in returning home the other was

One of the many sets of false identity papers, produced for
Maria in the spring of 1944

desperate. Our varied selection of false identity cards we kept nailed inside the wood of the back of the mirror in our room and we used to open this sometimes during the night. (Yes one can even learn to be a real gangster when necessary.) There was a clandestine Jewish organisation here from which Sigbert received a monthly subsidy, a jacket and a pair of trousers (which did not last very long) and I received the subsidy from the Swiss Legation but it was not nearly enough to live on. We did not know what to do for money – everything was terribly expensive – especially as we were paying for being hidden. I wanted to start teaching English again but Sigbert thought it was too dangerous – all my old pupils were begging me to and the price for English lessons was very high. I did start again with one or two of my most trusted pupils, but not for long as I knew too many people in Rome, and it was impossible to go out without meeting people at every step (rather like Anne in Chichester one evening: 'Oh let's go to Woolworths and meet all the people we know'). We disguised ourselves – Sigbert grew a horrible walrus moustache and never went out without a hat pulled down over his eyes (he was still wearing the old mackintosh that we had slept on every night in the Grotto). I wore my hair in several different ways – sometimes in plaits – and different hats and hair nets and an enormous pair of dark glasses, and when we went out Sigbert would say, 'Now don't look all round trying to see people you know – look down on the ground.' So I had to do what Anne and I used to do if we saw someone coming we didn't want to meet – look the other way and pretend I hadn't seen. — We knew nothing about Lewis. Every now and then we packed up a parcel and got it to him through the Swiss Legation but we could get no word to him at all. The Jewish organisation worked from America through the Vatican City and was run by a lovely old monk called Padre Benedetto – so kind and innocent-looking with long brown tunic, sandals and bare feet and long black beard and glasses. So calm and holy-looking but it was he who made false documents and he who cleaned away all writing on incriminating documents. — Then there was my Birthday. Oh you must know about that, even if it takes up too much space because it is lovely. Well in the middle of the night of the 29th Sigbert became very restless and said he didn't feel well. Then he got out of bed to go to the bathroom and became rather grumpy when I asked if I could do anything for him. This grumpiness usually means 'Leave me alone', so I did. With a grim face and looking as if he was going to be sick at any moment he left the room without looking to the right or left. Later I heard him move about in the kitchen and I sat up in bed trying to keep awake till he came back – but I couldn't and I slept till 5.30. Then it was lovely. He came back to bed and everything was grey and hazy and difficult to see and what one did see might or might not have been my imagination. I was drowsily half asleep and what I saw might have been a dream – but gradually things took form – yes, there *was* a table by my bed – with round and square and oblong things on it, and there *was* the most beautiful vase of daffodils and narcissus, and then the colours became clear – yellow and white, and white and gold, and gold and blue, and blue and red, and the parcels looked so exciting and it was so difficult to know what to open first. It was all so exciting but the most lovely things of all were the round flat things I opened last – gramophone records which he had made especially for my Birthday. After not having sung for six months, after having passed three months in an open Grotto, after the type of life we had been leading – the first time he tries out his voice is to make records! He made those records under dangerous circumstances for it was the 23rd of March and while he was singing there were loud explosions just under his window – for the Via Rasella incident was taking place and Sigbert was singing just near that street (you must have read of the hand bomb that was thrown into a group of Germans, killing 32 – for which the day after 320 Italians were shot in the Ardeatina Caves just out-side Rome). Sigbert could not look out of the window – Germans were shooting everywhere and anywhere (on one of the records you can hear Sigbert's voice shaking) and all the houses were blocked. Nobody could go in or out and Germans were entering all the houses examining identity documents. Sigbert was sure they would look at his, was sure they would know it was false and there seemed no way out, until an Italian soldier opened a door into a back street and said to Sigbert and one or two others, 'Get out quickly!' Sigbert almost fell out into the street – but right into the arms of the Head of the Political Police who knows Sigbert and us well after all our negotiations last year to keep Sigbert in Rome and then for us to go to Picinisco. He gave Sigbert one look and turned in the opposite direction. So that we escaped too. Yes, those were awful days. We always imagined someone was following us – we never dared look anyone in the face, always trying to pretend we were what we weren't, always imagining we were being glanced at suspiciously, always trying to avoid being known or becoming conspicuous in any way (the only coat I had not lost was my lovely old fuschia coat which was really at the end of its life but I immediately had it dyed black and started to wear it again); always guarding our words and thinking twice before we spoke and to whom and then being annoyed with ourselves after-wards for perhaps having said too much or given some-thing away; never writing anything on any piece of paper; always memorising telephone numbers; not owning any-thing that was written either in English or German –

in fact pretending not to understand those languages (once when our landlady, Signora Chierichetti, was listening in to some English on the radio, she said 'what language is that?' and I said 'French'); never giving our address to anybody – we used to tell our friends we just changed round from place to place every two or three days. And sometimes we became really desperate and without hope of surviving this – it seemed just a question of rather unlikely luck. There we were living in the centre of Germans – a German nest – a Jew and an English girl living together pretending to be married, with false identity and ration cards, both being searched for, Sigbert in mass form and me personally with photographs, and all our old addresses being in the hands of the police, and Lewis in prison... Our situation seemed hopeless and we had to bribe several people and we had no money, and I knew too many people in Rome and they were always trying to find me, and we were well known by the police from before, and the Germans had a horrible habit of raiding the houses at night just to see who was who and they had experts at proving false documents and they used to look in every cupboard and under the beds, because half Rome was in hiding for one reason or another – either because they were foreigners or Jews or Italians who had deserted or refused to be called under arms – most people had different names and different addresses and the German

S.S. police were very clever at picking up these people and taking them to Via Tasso [the famous German torturing chambers in the centre of Rome]. By the way if you hear any stories of Via Tasso you can multiply them and not subtract from them because everything you may hear is true and worse. (Since the 4th June we have talked to several people we know who have experienced it, including Signora Venet's son of Via Babuino – our landlady of last year – who showed me her son's torn and bloody clothes. He was often pierced all over his body with a stiletto and had two ribs broken and was beaten. Other people had their teeth pulled out to make them speak – oh, and other terrible things.) We were sure they would come to our house – we were so much in the centre and in the midst of the Commands, and we could not find another room; and then lists were made as to the inmates of every flat and every house, and these lists were pasted up at the entrance of every house liable to control at any moment. With difficulty we kept our names from going on any of these lists. Then there was the difficulty of buying bread because every name, address, and number of identity card had to be registered at the baker's in order to be able to buy bread – this was a kind of trick to test false documents. In the end the Cavalier of Pensione Nella came to the rescue and included our ration cards with those of the Pensione so again we succeeded in avoiding giving our address anywhere. Then one day in the beginning of April, Sigbert and Esther went to Signora Venet to find some shoes of mine, and she greeted them by saying, 'Tell Signora Leslie not to let herself be seen – the German S.S. come here every day looking for her. They have large photographs of her, and I always say I haven't seen her.' After that Sigbert insisted on me staying indoors, which I did with great difficulty for seven weeks. It was really difficult in that lovely spring weather being cooped up in that tiny little room and afterwards I was so weak I could hardly walk. If it had not been for Sigbert, of course, I could not have done it – he made me do it – and if it had not been for Sigbert I should not be here now because only after the 4th June did we discover just to what extent they had been looking for me. Every day without ever tiring they would go to Signora Venet, the Morettis' house and the Abbate family and there they would stay for hours on end being sure that one day I would turn up. They told Mrs Moretti they would arrest her if she did not say where I was (fortunately she didn't know). With the Venets and the Abbates they would sit in the kitchen watching the door every time it opened – and they said they wanted to shoot me as I was a very dangerous spy. But at the time we did not know that and only Sigbert imagined it. Sigbert was so nice during all those hard weeks, cheering me up and bringing me lovely surprises – new books and cakes and ices (which were very difficult to find), and he went almost daily to the famous black market of Rome, Tor di Nona, and I never knew what he was going to bring back next! It was so exciting. But I was never in peace while he was out; in fact we were never in peace at all in those days with German atrocities going on all round us. By that time we had many debts, and Sigbert had made many contracts for exchange of dollars in America, for we were obliged to live completely by the black market, buying flour at £2.3.0 a kilo, meat at £3.10.0 a kilo, butter at £8.0.0 a kilo and so on, when these things could be found. Through Peppino and Elsa Imesch of the Vatican we had got to know Montgomery of the British Legation to the Vatican. He was very kind to us and gave money to me and secured some money for Sigbert from the Pope. So we continued hoping for the best but feeling it was rather useless to hope. Nothing seemed to be happening on the front. They were still battling round Cassino – they had been doing it when we were in the Grotto. The Anzio question seemed to be still [ie the Germans were stopping the Allies from advancing] and nobody seemed to be hopeful that the Allies would soon arrive in Rome – and if they did what would happen first in Rome? What last desperate effort would the Germans make before leaving? Would they destroy Rome? Would they go into every house systematically for the men? Everybody was frightened and every time the front door-bell rang one expected the worst. Once they did come to our house: fortunately Sigbert was out and I was in bed not well, but, though three of them came into our room and looked into the cupboards, they were not searching for us that time but for a Jew who had lived in the room before us (we had already got rid of all his documents, some of which would have been quite incriminating to him.) Kept my nerve, dear, and said yes, yes, I was feeling *awfully* sick – sooner they left me the better, sort of thing. — Then, all of a sudden, the Cassino offensive started and the front began to advance quickly. Rome was in a fever. Nobody dared look or speak to anyone and the Germans increased their arrests and torture – Italians were ordered to join the Army and move North; few of them did, and the others risked death in Rome – waiting in something like the same tenseness as we were. Then it was given out that severe reprisals were going to be taken on May the 25th for all men who hadn't joined up. There were rumours that houses would be surrounded at midnight and the men would be forced to come out of the houses. We got nervous as our house would have been one of the first – and the front was advancing really this time. We *must* save ourselves for the last moment – they mustn't catch us now – we could even hear the first cannons [ie the Allies were arriving]. Oh, if *only* they would arrive – it seemed the biggest joy imaginable – we dared not hope or think. Sigbert had the idea of sending me to some out of the way Convent, and he himself hiding where he could, but I couldn't bear that idea – it would be awful to be separated in the midst of this desperation. But what could we do? How could we remain hidden till the end? Then, as usual we had luck. One Sunday about the middle of May, Sigbert was discussing our situation with a friend of his, and this friend said, 'But you are very lucky – you both have friends in the Vatican. Why don't you go there for these last few weeks?' Peppino and Elsa Imesch. We would never dare ask them such a thing. How could we? They were living in a neutral state under a neutral law and nobody from Rome was allowed to stay in the Vatican. But Sigbert was desperately worried and suddenly he decided that everything must be tried. In this spirit he left his friend, went straight to a Café to telephone to the Vatican, wanting to see them immediately as in that psychological moment he felt he could explain everything exactly and they must understand and be convinced. He telephoned but there was no answer – evidently they were out. He put down the receiver and turning round he saw Peppino and Elsa Imesch entering the Café! — We believe the Gods were with us, for that moment was our fortune. (You see it is very strange to see those two in Rome as they hardly ever leave the Vatican.) That was the moment which saved us. Sigbert poured out everything, explaining that it was life or death for us now, and they listened and then confessed that they already had two people in a similar condition to us whom they had promised several months ago to hide at the last moment – but only at the last moment. These two people had arrived the day before. Peppino laughed and said, 'But if we have two we may as well have four. When do you want to come?' Sigbert returned that evening as if he was drunk. He flung himself into the room and for some moments he could not speak. I could not imagine what had happened, and then it came out. 'We are saved – we are saved – we are going to live. Tomorrow we are going into the Vatican till the Allies arrive.' The next morning we went and we had to enter the Vatican carefully and with few parcels so as just to look as if we were on an ordinary afternoon visit, and when we got there we had to be more than ever careful, for nobody must know. And we were four extra people in the house – the others were a Napolitan lawyer of a political nature who had been put in prison by the Germans and was continually being searched for by the S.S. and the girl who lived with him: Amedeo and Lina. We had to walk about on tiptoe as the floors and walls were very thin and every movement could be heard by the Swiss soldiers underneath; we had to talk in whispers, never look out of the windows, and disappear into one room if the front door bell rang. Peppino's career would have been finished if we had been discovered there. Sigbert and I slept in the dining-room – there was a sofa and a mattress on the floor. The sofa was terribly noisy and every time I moved only one arm I was sure the soldiers underneath could hear. Sigbert would say, 'Don't make such an awful noise. Move quietly, can't you?' but I had hardly moved at all! We stayed there two weeks and during that time we slept, read and I taught English to Sigbert, Amedeo and Lina. Amedeo was continually annoying us, being one of those tiresome men who will bring out the same phrase over and over again on every possible occasion and then expect everyone to laugh. His stock phrase was '*Forza Giorgio!*' (which I suppose is translated by 'At him George!') and this came out when-ever an aeroplane passed, whenever anybody dropped anything, whenever I asked somebody a question during an English lesson, whenever the radio started up, when-ever anybody knocked on the door etc and whenever he said it he rose majestically to his full height and started conducting an imaginary orchestra. Ludicrous man... We began to get nervously excited. We listened to the English and American Radio every few hours and we heard how quickly the Allies were advancing towards Rome. Cannons were firing near us all the time – it was heavenly. I never knew it was possible to love the sound of cannons, but for us it was music. I remember some nights that I did not sleep at all and the cannons continued all night, not stopping even for five minutes and the house was shaking and every shot seemed to be louder and nearer. It was a blessed sound. I have never longed to see the Union Jack so much in my life – to see an English face – but more than all to feel safe again. We could not imagine what that must be like. We were so used to being chased about everywhere like criminals that we had forgotten what it was like to hold up our heads and look somebody in the face. Then the Allies took Frosinone, and joined up with the Anzio front, Valmontone, but by then I especially had grown too pessimistic and even when they arrived at the Albion Hills I did not believe they were really going to take Rome! On Sunday the 4th June, Peppino was down at the Vatican gates talking to the retiring German soldiers – mostly young boys who had come on foot from Valmontone and who had not slept for eight days, dragging themselves along in broken files with their legs covered with blood, and they were taking away any cars, bicycles, carts, buses or likely transport object they could find. One of them said to Peppino, 'Oh, the English will be here by midnight tonight. We know all you Romans are just longing for their arrival, but you wait. Well the English aren't really so bad but the Americans are terrible and you will never have a moment's peace.' (As if we had had peace with them.) And it was just about midnight on that Sunday night when the first American troops came into Rome. But we did not leave the Vatican till early Monday morning when we staggered into the streets dazed and happy, Sigbert for the first time without a hat and lovely smooth face because he had shaved away that horrid moustache and I with my hair loose again and nothing to hide me. How everlastingly grateful we shall be to Peppino and Elsa Imesch who were so kind and generous to us and saved us completely – for we learnt later that two days after we had left Via Veneto to go to the Vatican the German S.S. had traced me there. They had gone to Signora Chierichetti and said there was a foreigner living in her house by the name of Mary Gill. She was able to say quite truthfully that she had no foreigners and knew nobody by that name. But to this day we can't imagine how they knew I was there, for nobody knew our address, I had been living indoors all the time and there I was believed to be Italian. Fortunately, they had not connected Gill-Leslie-Santarelli as being the same person. — We came out of the Vatican on the morning of the 5th feeling completely new-born – in fact we call June 5th 'Our Birthday'. The whole of Rome had come out into the streets; crowds everywhere cheering on the American and English lorries, everybody gay and shouting to every-body else and Allied soldiers everywhere talking and laughing; and the English language was the strangest thing I had heard for a long time. It seemed as if all these soldiers had somewhere learnt to speak English awfully well. It took us some time to get used to the feeling of being free and for some time after we still remained Tino and Maria Santarelli – in fact, some people will always call us by these names out of sheer habit. — We were worried about Lewis. What could have happened to him? One of two things – either he had been taken up to the North by the Germans or he had succeeded in getting out of prison on the last day with some Italian political prisoners… We spent that lovely happy day celebrating with Esther and Sandro. We were alive. We had Won – and all the German S.S. in the world had not succeeded in shooting us. What did it matter if we had lost all our possessions? What did it matter if Sigbert had no pants and I no night-dress? No shirts, socks, stockings, underclothes, overclothes, nothing. No, nothing mattered – we were alive and we kept telling each other so just to remind ourselves of the fact, because it still seemed so incredible. We laughed a lot that day, and towards evening, lazy with happiness, we made our way towards home – home being our tiny room in Via Veneto where we had been hidden all these months. On the way we talked to lots of soldiers who gave us chocolate and cigarettes – things we hadn't seen for a long time. Then, all of a sudden we ran into Guido, and he said, 'Oh, have you heard the news?' We laughed and said of course we had, we could see it all round us in these heavenly tanks that were passing every moment. 'Oh no,' he said, 'I mean that Lewis is at my house!' Oh, so Lewis was free too! After five months of prison. But Lewis's rejoicing could not be the same as ours, for we realised the moment had come to tell him everything. Poor Lewis. What could we do? We could not pretend any longer, things had to be faced and yet to hurt Lewis so terribly after five months of prison? We thought out several ideas but none of them seemed to help us. Should I go back to Lewis for one or two months till he had got used to life again and then break it to him gradually? No, that would be more cruel in the end. Besides, I could never make him happy and that was a compromise which would not help any of us; and anyway Sigbert and I just could not separate now. What we had wanted for a long time had come about by a natural kind of process and I was convinced there was no way out. Sigbert and I went that same evening and had dinner with Lewis at Guido's house. We heard all Lewis's story which was that on the morning of the 7th January, the day we all left Picinisco, he had overtaken the Berents on the road and had travelled with them in a German lorry as far as Sora where he had continued walking by himself. On arriving near Frosinone he had asked the driver of another lorry to give him a lift to Rome. By chance a German officer happened to be looking out of the window of a nearby cottage and, recognising Lewis to be English, had asked him for his identity papers. Lewis, seeing it was no good pretending, showed his English passport, and the officer said, 'Come with me.' Lewis spent two days in prison at Frosinone, where they treated him very well and gave him plenty to eat, then they took him in a private car to Rome telling him that everything would go well, that they had just the right kind of camps for him in Germany – and a pity his wife wasn't with him, too. But when he reached Rome it was a very different story and the trouble started when they found the document given by the interpreter at Picinisco written in German and saying that Lewis was Italian. They immediately thought he was a spy and wanted to know all details about how Lewis received the document. Lewis had to lie in order not to compromise the interpreter, and in a second interview they put him through the third degree in which Lewis said he had been to the Municipal Building to get the documents with everyone else, that they had been given out almost in mass when the village was ordered to evacuate. — 'Oh,' said they, 'what was the room in this building like? What did the man look like who wrote it? Was he wearing glasses?' At the end of a long interview, during which the officer was very rude to Lewis, they told him they knew the interpreter had given him the document and if Lewis said one word of denial he would be shot with the interpreter. Well the interpreter was shot, and Lewis was pushed into a separate cell where he was listed as a very dangerous person and he had to give the addresses of Pensione Nella, the Abbate family, Signora Venet, and the hotel where we had left our packing cases. He did not give the Moretti address even though the S.S. had told Mrs Moretti that Lewis had said that I was sure to be hiding in one or other of Rosanna's flats. He was alone in a cell for two months with just wishy-washy prison soups and bread and the parcels from the Swiss Legation. He spent the last three months in a cell with another English prisoner by the name of Armstrong and things were a bit better. He used to sing scales and exercises at the top of his voice for about two hours every day – could be heard all over the prison, and the warder brought him a guitar (which he still has) so he played most of the day and composed a march for an officer and spoke English with his companion – something which Lewis has always missed doing. On the day before the arrival of the Allies in Rome, a German officer came to the cell and said, 'Leslie, pick up your things and come with me – quickly, there's no time to lose.' (Now what's going to happen, thought Lewis). He was taken into the courtyard and bundled into a large lorry presumably to be taken up North, but after a short distance the lorry stopped and he was taken out and put into a small private car which took him to a private house, still in Rome. There, they went up in a lift, and Lewis thought that rather good after Grottos and prisons, and then into a room which had an air of secrecy and where people hardly spoke to each other. After about half a day a German officer said to Lewis, 'Have you many friends in Rome?' and Lewis, thinking that might be a trick, replied guardingly, 'Well, I've been here for some time so naturally I made acquaintances.' 'Very good,' said the officer and went away. Towards evening a French woman came to him and told him in so many words that he was free and could go when he wanted. Gradually, Lewis understood that this was the work of one or two German S.S. in conjunction with Italian partisans, and that he was really free, so he went straight to Guido's house, and together they watched the entrance of the Allies into Rome. After hearing Lewis's story we told ours, though we did not tell him the full story till the next day when I returned alone and confessed everything to Lewis, starting from four and a half years ago. Oh dear, it is so terrible to have to tell you in a letter all the words and conversations which have followed that day, all the terrible unhappiness of Lewis and how I hate to hurt him so. His reactions, of course, have different phases – poor Lewis, he is trying to think straight and fathom out the reason of it all, when really these things cannot be measured in reason at all. At first, he said he had known about it all for a long time and had not said anything because he had such complete faith in me, and he said he would divorce me and try and return to England as soon as possible. Though he said the worst part of the suffering was over – because he had imagined it all in the Grotto and the prison – I saw he was terribly broken. (You see even to say this is not enough because they are just words in comparison to what Lewis felt and feels.) My only hope is that with time it will be able to heal... Then he became rather fierce and said I had committed a downright crime, out of weakness and just for the fun of playing with fire – that from the beginning I should have resisted and not broken up a happy marriage. He says that it is all my fault and I must be punished for doing a wicked thing. I must be really unhappy in order that it may bring me back in the end to real happiness. Then sometimes he says it is all Sigbert's fault because he should have gone away right at the beginning or anyway never have returned to Rome; and Lewis thinks that Sigbert has been wickedly hypocritical to pretend such friendship to him, for no real friend could do what he has done. But that is wrong because Sigbert's friendship as I have said before was real and genuine and that is what made it so difficult also for him. Then sometimes Lewis says it is his own fault because he should have seen to it that it was stamped out in the beginning in order to protect our marriage. He says that I am blind and running into danger without seeing it, that I can never be happy as I shall always have this great sin on my conscience, and how *could* I do such a thing. Even if Jesus

Christ had come down on to the earth and asked me to go away with him I should have to refuse and say, 'No, I am already married' (and Jesus Christ would have said to himself, 'Yes, she's right.') Then Lewis told Sigbert he must go away immediately and never come back again. Then he made a proposal that I should go back and live with him for five months without ever seeing Sigbert for he said he knew with time I should return to him as before. But I refused this proposal. What was the use? I could not make Lewis happy and he would suffer even more seeing that I wanted to be with Sigbert all the time. And Sigbert could not go away because then all three of us would be miserable without doing any good to anyone – and anyway this was no longer possible for us – we *had* to live together. — We continued living in Via Veneto and Lewis stayed with Guido for two weeks, then found a room (only about two minutes from us) in Via Toscana 30. We both got jobs. Lewis works in the P.W.B. mostly during the night, as a kind of newspaper editor. I work in the A.M.G. as secretary to the Chief Legal Officer for Rome and provinces, who is extremely nice and kind. I do all the technical translations from Italian into English and vice versa, including regional and administrative orders. I have not seen Lewis for several weeks – partly also because he works all night and I work all day. — And Rosanna? Well, she stayed in prison for three months and was then sentenced to death, but by luck she happened to know the wife of the judge and by some trick got out of prison, but the S.S. continued to follow her and she was often taken to the police station where they tried to force her to say where her father was hiding. Naturally before the 4th June we could not meet, but after I was so anxious and glad to see her, but I found she was almost indifferent – not I think really because she feels less friendly but because she is living with a man to whom she says she is engaged and this takes up all her thoughts. Well she hadn't even time to help me find the remnants of my clothes which were left in her flat and though Sigbert and I went there several days she couldn't really be bothered or was too busy or was always going to do it the next day. She didn't seem to understand that I needed everything so badly. She too has lost many things but has already been able to re-stock her wardrobe. Sigbert and I are just at rock-bottom (as Brenda would say). Sigbert has lost absolutely *everything* – all his music, all his books, all his clothes, all photos and letters and documents – every single possession was stolen. He has only one pair of trousers, one jacket and a mackintosh and one pair of shoes and practically nothing else. It is impossible to find anything in Rome and if one does the prices are quite impossible. One day we returned to Picinisco (we saw Cassino which is nothing but a sinisterly picturesque mass of bricks) – hitch-hiking, and we found that everything we had left in the well had also been stolen, so now we have no winter clothes at all – two overcoats of mine stolen (one of which was quite new and I had never worn), nine almost new jumpers stolen and all my skirts and winter dresses. I found some of my summer dresses with Rosanna and three silk materials which I have now had made up, but alas soon the summer will be over. And Sigbert and I? We are happy and we are free, but our life is still unsatisfactory at the moment. I work in the office from 8 o'clock in the morning till 6 o'clock in the evening with just a lunch hour in the middle of the day. I return home in the evening tired and incapable of doing anything. Meanwhile, poor Sigbert has to do all the things that I should do – all the stupid little domestic details which normally do not take much time but which in these days with all the difficulties take all day – prenoting ration cards, cutting off coupons and getting a few grams of sugar; standing in a queue in the boiling sun to buy fruit; trailing over to the Vatican to get our clothes washed because here in Rome they ruin everything with chemicals; walking backwards and forwards to various shops trying to get together something for our evening meal, for we never know from day to day what we are going to eat there being so little food in Rome, and the rations being almost non-existent we have to buy on the black market when we can find things. All this takes it out of him so much – he walks round Rome all day in this awful heat, for there are hardly any trams and no buses, that of course he has no time and energy to sing. And that is terrible as he has not sung since last October except to make the records for me and every now and then for friends, and now is the moment to start his career again. He is 35 and must not lose any more time as his career has been continually broken into for the last ten years and now the opera houses etc, are making up their winter programmes. All his friends say to him, 'Now we are all free, when are you going to give a concert?' and he has to answer that he is not singing at the moment, the reason being of course that he has to scrape together the food. We both need time to get down to our life again, and begin the reconstructing process. I have not sung since 1943 July – over a year and I dare not think if I have a voice still or not – and how long will it take me to finish my studying now? Probably years and years after this long interruption. And we are both tired and undernourished and Sigbert is very thin having lost 20 kilos since four years ago… About four weeks ago (the date today being August the 25th) we had the most heavenly surprise. One evening about nine o'clock our landlady told me there was an officer to see me. I went out and who do you think it was?? PATRICK!!!!! You can't imagine what I felt in that moment. He said he felt as if Max, Priscilla, Mary and Anne were walking in the door at the same moment, and I felt the same. (He had found my address through the A.M.G. [Allied Military Government], having worried the life out of the police in Naples and all the way up through South Italy, and he had found my name on German S.S. lists). There he was standing there in uniform – Captain Brawn – taller than he was five years ago and a good bit thinner. I spent the next two hours pouring out the story I have told you in this letter and he said such nice things and was so understanding and we talked a lot about you and it was heavenly. Patrick has his office in Rome now and it happens to be in the same building as Lewis and also he is staying in the same hotel where Lewis eats so they see each other often and we see Patrick often – we all work and live within two minutes of each other. Patrick and Sigbert get on very well and they have the common language of German. When we are together Patrick and Sigbert speak German, Patrick and I speak English, and Sigbert and I speak Italian. Patrick and I spent one heavenly Sunday afternoon reading your letters (which fortunately the Germans didn't steal). We read through every one and it was a bit like being with you again. We shrieked with laughter for about 20 minutes on end when we read your letter, Priscilla, about your dream that Mr Brawn was a boiled ham!. — I think I will leave Patrick to tell you about all his conversations with Lewis for he can see it all from a clearer point of view having come in from outside as it were, and besides I find Patrick is a person of extraordinarily clear vision. Whatever *I* tell you is naturally biased. I can tell you about our happiness, Sigbert and I: I can tell you about Lewis's great unhappiness for he feels his life is broken and not worthwhile any more, as if the whole foundation has been taken away – sometimes he feels he just wants to hide and not see anybody and other times he feels he wants to strike out for his future, divorce me, marry again and make a family, and other times he thinks that perhaps after all I shall return to him. Poor Lewis. How terrible it is to have to hurt a person so deeply. Patrick said to me once, 'If I had been Sigbert I would have done what Sigbert has done; if I had been you I would have done what you have done; but if I had been Lewis I would have shot Sigbert.' — Sigbert and I want to marry as soon as Lewis will divorce me which he says he will do immediately he returns to England. We have no plans for the future yet but the most important thing is that Sigbert must sing and sing and sing. The first thing we must do is to get out of the mess we are in at the moment and then begin to build up our life again. At least we are FREE and ALIVE... But Sigbert has another great sadness which I have not told you about. In June 1942 he received a card from his mother who was still living in Berlin and from whom he had received letters regularly while he was in the Concentration Camp, who said, 'I can't write to you any more as tomorrow I have to leave and I don't know where I am going.' Sigbert only knows that she was taken to a Concentration Camp in Poland and he has heard nothing since. He always hopes but it is so terrible to think of all the things they have done and are doing to Jews in Poland. He seldom talks about it but I know how much he feels... As I said in the beginning of this letter, don't make hasty judgments about all I have told you. This is only a letter of facts and there is so much to be explained by voice. I have so much to tell you, so many things which can't be written, but so many things which you *must* understand. I long and long to speak to you and tell you everything. Sigbert and I would love to come back to England but so far we do not know how this can be done. Patrick is making enquiries here and Max, *please*, could you do the same in London, taking into consideration that Sigbert is what they call here *'Apolide'* which means completely without nationality and a bearer of the Nansen passport (which he has not got now as it was taken from him when he was interned). He only had the Romanian nationality while he could remain on his father's passport and afterwards he never took the German or any other nationality. Both his parents were Romanian but he was born in Berlin where he has always lived. I *long* and *long* and *long* to see you so much and be with you again in England.

***

14th September 1944 — Now I have finished this
letter which I started on the 4th July and which has
been written at all odd intervals, sometimes on
Patrick's typewriter and sometimes in the office.
Since finishing it several other things have happened
and, of course, will continue to happen till this
letter goes off. Unfortunately, Patrick has left Rome
and he was going to show me all his letters from you
when his luggage arrived and the book on Eric. He
told me that Eric is dead which I did not know and I
am very sorry about it because I should so like to
have seen him again. I had Anne's heavenly letter
two days ago and I am waiting all the time for one
from you. I have been made a Lieutenant now and I
am called an Executive Assistant though I don't have
to wear uniform. (I am hoping it will mean I can eat
a bit better.) And Sigbert *will* insist on saluting me
when we wake up in the morning or last thing at
night or when we meet in the street! I want to tell
you more about Lewis. He is much better in every
sense; everybody says so, including Patrick.
Physically he is looking strong, fat and fit and
spiritually he is not suffering nearly so much and he

himself admits that he is getting over it. He is working very hard both in P.W.B. and at music and that is a good thing. I do *hope* he will be happy again soon. Please write as *soon* as you can and a *long* letter – and if it is allowed send photos of you all. I should be mad with joy to see them.

I send you my fondest love,

Mary

Maria and Sigbert, Rome, 1946

Maria and Sigbert on a return visit
to the grotto above Picinisco, 1946

Rome-ance 'roun th world

LOVE FINDS WAY—A romance that started in June, 3), in Rome and was interrupted for three years by the war, ended happily yesterday r Joan-Mary Leslie of London and Robert Corell, Romanian concert singer. They ry married in Judge P. James Pellecchia's office in a double-ring wedding.

Press cuttings of Maria
and Sigbert's marriage,
New York, 1947

Terrors of War End in Wedding

Students Hid in Italian Cave, United Here

An 8-year courtship, hindered by internment and highlighted by a stay in an Italian cave, flight with a price on their heads and final safety in Vatican City, ended with the wedding yesterday in Police Judge Pellecchia's office of an English girl and a Romanian.

Miss Joan-Mary Leslie, 26, of London and Robert Corell, 38, were the bride and bridegroom. They met in 1939 in Rome, where they were studying singing. At the outbreak of the War Corell was interned at Ferramenti. Later he was transferred to a camp at Piciniscio where Miss Leslie was held.

The latter camp was near Cassino and the prisoners escaped during the fierce fighting for the town. They fled to the mountains. A group of three men and two women, aided by friendly Italians, evaded capture for three months.

They made their way to Rome where they were aided at the Vatican. Corell came here six months ago and Miss Leslie arrived late in April. They are staying with friends of her family in Forest Hills, L. I.

6 MMM · 1947.

form the double-ring wedding.

MET IN JUNE, 1939

It started in June, 1939, when Joan-Mary, a small, dark-eyed brunette, met Corell in Rome, where she was studying music and he was singing. When war broke out, both were interned and for nearly three years, until they were transferred to a village camp near the Monte Cassino abbey, saw nothing of each other.

About a year after being interned together, they managed to escape. For three months they hided with a German Gestapo by the

DREAMS

Between July 1943 and December 1944 — 'a period of fear, hunger and survival' — Maria Corelli had many nightmares which she meticulously recorded the moment after she awoke. Some of the most significant of these are included below:

20th July 1943 — Rome

Air Raid Alarm – and immediately the sky is full of aeroplanes. Bombs are falling while the siren is still sounding. Lewis, Sigbert and I are in the doorway of a house. Other people arrive because they say this is an English house and therefore will not be hit by the bombs. In fact it is 'South Nore' ('South Nore' in the middle of Rome!) With joy I recognise the house and am amazed to find it here. Bombs are falling close to us and we can see many dead people. The cemetery is also near and many graves have been bombed open. People are shouting – wild cries like animals. We look up at the sky – it is raining bombs – they are falling all around us but miraculously they do not hit us. Sigbert and I, hand in hand, go out and we arrive at a wall where there are many dead people lying about. We see a wounded donkey crying with one paw raised in the air. Sigbert takes his handkerchief from his pocket and bandages the donkey's leg, then he strokes his forehead.

Suddenly we hear a tremendous, inhuman, mechanical shriek. In fact we have only just time to run back to the house before a whole squadron of English aeroplanes drives through the street, just like so many motor cars. It is a horrible sight – one after another they dash rapidly along with a frightful thundering noise. Where there are people they are mown down like so many pieces of grass. The wings shine sinisterly in the sun and the long line of infernal birds seems as if it will never finish. But finally the last one passes and they can be seen only in the distance above the mountains. I notice that all the windows of South Nore are broken.

22nd July 1943 — Rome

Lewis and I are in a house in Picinisco. The floor of the house is nothing but loose earth and there is no furniture. We can hear the roar of an aeroplane and we know that it is a plane that wants to bomb us. It flies round our house for quite a long time. Every moment we are waiting for the bombs to fall. We get close together and hide our heads in the ground like two storks. Lewis says, 'if our cheeks touch we shall die together'. — 'Yes, that is much better,' I answer. We continue to wait for the inevitable bomb, but instead, the aeroplane comes down and perches on the roof of our house. We look up and see that the propeller of the plane has got stuck in the doorway. The English pilot gets out and asks for some water. 'We hid in the ground to avoid the bombs,' we tell him and he answers, 'Yes, it is the only way of saving oneself.'

27th August 1943 — Rome

One evening, Auntie Eva, Anne, Lewis and I are discussing where we can eat. Eva has come from Via Tronto, where she lives, especially to eat with us. Finally we decide to go to a restaurant nearby, in via Babuino. We eat well and there is also meat. We decide we will eat here also tomorrow for lunch. Eva says, 'Yes, all right. I will spend the night in a bookshop near here where I want to buy some books – in that way I shall save myself the journey to via Tronto.' We think this is a good idea. Then Lewis asks for some jam because he has some bread left, and I ask for some butter, so we eat butter and jam together. Then the waiter brings us some raspberries with cream and sugar. What a joy! They are in a large glass bowl and are a beautiful colour. He also brings us some little plates of dark glass to eat them on. We are very happy. But we look at the time and see that it is nearly curfew time. Fortunately we are near home but it is already 10.25. Then it occurs to me that Eva has to pass the night in a bookshop and will probably be hungry during the night. So I prepare some more raspberries on other plates for Eva. I pour out the cream and sugar. I am having a lovely time –

they are so beautifully red and make me think back to other days. But the minutes are passing. Lewis says 'Be quick, you can't play about with curfew – they take it seriously.' Yes, yes – but just two more raspberries, there, there, they look so nice and just a little more cream and sugar otherwise they don't taste good. Now they are ready to give to Eva. But now it is twenty to eleven – ten minutes late! I think to myself that Sigbert would have said 'Mamma mia!' (Gosh!). Eva and Anne have gone, not being able to wait any longer. I run after them with the raspberries. I cannot see them but I hear them in the distance. I shout 'Anne, Anne, take these,' and louder still 'Anne, Anne!' I know she can hear me but does not want to come back and this annoys me. Suddenly on the path in front of me three men appear – two soldiers and one plain clothes man. The latter has a gun in his hand and he raises it and shoots. Instinctively I put my hand over my heart for protection and fall to the ground with a shout. The glass plate of the raspberries is smashed to pieces and I lie motionless. I can feel the blood running down my fingers, hot and sticky, but I feel no pain. I wonder if I am dead, but I don't think so. I think to myself that Lewis must have heard either the shout or the shot, so why doesn't he come? Ah no, Lewis will be thinking that it is useless for two people to die if it is not necessary. This is quite right and I think Lewis very sensible. In *the meantime the three men are looking at me – they want to see if I am dead so that they will leave me and go on.*

2nd September 1943 — Rome

We are in the bus going quickly to Piazza del Popolo where in a few minutes the Pope is going to make a speech from the steps of Piazza del Popolo, and all Romans must be present. There is a great feeling of expectation and hope in the air. We have arrived and the obelisk is surrounded by people. The Pope appears in the centre all dressed in white and Rosanna and I sit on a high step one each side of him, because Rosanna says it would be ridiculous to sit in deck-chairs. Other buses arrive full of people who crowd round the monument waiting anxiously for the Pope's words. He raises his hand and blesses the people, then he begins his speech. He speaks of peace and then says, 'to show we are good Italians we will make the corn come', and suddenly lots of yellow war cars arrive. They dash wildly round the square in circles dropping grains of corn from the bottom of the cars as if they were watering the street. The people all look amazed while the cars go round quicker and quicker and the whole square becomes one thick, wide carpet of yellow corn. Rosanna laughs maliciously and says: 'Now you can't cross the square, Mary, you must wait until the end. Anyway you won't die.'

5th October 1943 — Picinisco (*in hiding in Grotto*)

Sigbert has gone out and shortly after I go out towards the village. I get as far as the blacksmith's when I hear the noise of a car. A man shows me the direction of Atina but very close to Picinisco a German motor cycle, which is travelling by electric wires like the Roman buses, crosses a long field. It stops and the driver gets off and speaks to some other nearby German soldiers. The man with me tells me to wait while he goes to see what they want. I watch him going away and then speaking with the Germans. After a bit he comes back running, but he is not kind any more as he was before – the expression on his face has changed and he seems very hostile towards me. He says, 'The Germans have to come to take away the English internees and I have the job of taking these to him. So come with me and we will go and fetch your husband.' We go back to our house and I ask him to wait outside while I go and find Lewis. He says, 'Hurry up then.' As soon as I get inside I lock the door and we all decide to escape out of the little bathroom door at the back. The two Berents and Lewis go on ahead and I wait behind the house for Sigbert. I hide behind the bushes hoping that Sigbert will not run into the man who is waiting for us outside. I hear the man's footsteps going up and down outside the house. At last Sigbert arrives carrying the basket containing the 'Nonna'. We climb up the slope behind the house and Sigbert slips down several times because the ground is wet. We walk for a long time without being sure where we are going. We are in a large wood and everything around is dark and wet. After some time we arrive at the Grotto and there we find Lewis with the Berents and Salstein and Nass. The Grotto seems full but Sigbert shouts out, 'there is room for everybody.' We see they have made a new road directly in front of the Grotto and this is very annoying as the passers by can see us. In fact almost continuously there are people passing by on the street, but strangely enough they never look inside the Grotto. Mrs Berent begins to chatter in an ever louder voice. Everybody tells her to be quiet but she won't listen. It seems as if she speaks louder on purpose wherever there is somebody outside. Sigbert gets angry and I cover her mouth with my hands pushing them down harder and harder.

19th October 1943 — Picinisco (in hiding in Grotto)
We are in the Grotto. Suddenly we hear a terrible shout like the howling of an animal. But this shout comes from Mrs Nass who is in Picinisco. It is such a heart-rending cry that I decide to go to Picinisco to see what is the matter. When I arrive at the village square I see a crowd of people including Germans and Mrs Nass who is crying and screaming. A procession is being formed – a funeral procession, and everybody is shouting in a monotonous and rhythmical voice, 'The Germans have killed Mr Nass.' In front there are some wagons which begin to move and the procession grows longer and longer. I go behind, ready to escape at the first moment – nobody is watching me. When the right moment comes I hide behind the bushes and watch the people passing guarded by the Germans who form sentinels on either side of the procession. I always hear the mechanical rhythm of the words – 'I tedeschi hanno ucciso il signor Nass!' 'The Germans have killed Mister Nass!'

22nd October 1943 — Picinisco (in hiding in Grotto)
Lewis, Sigbert and I are in a large garden with six other men. We hear the noise of a car and see a German lorry and a car passing. They come very close to us as one corner of the garden is open on to the street. We immediately crouch down in the grass near a wall, but the Germans

look down and see us. The driver of the lorry has dark hair and a long, thick, black moustache and he smiles ironically at us. When they have passed Sigbert says, 'Mary, are you under the impression that that moustache was real?' — I answer, 'No, it is probably stuck on' — 'With glue?' says Sigbert. 'Yes, for certain with glue.' Then I say, 'But I think having seen us the Germans will come and look for us.' 'But no', says Lewis, 'they haven't time.' 'But in any case it is better to be prepared', says Sigbert. So we decide to escape through the gate at the other side of the garden. We run towards it and find a closed door in front of the gate. Fortunately Lewis has the key and we have hardly got through the door when we see the Germans arrive in the garden. We run up the mountain among the trees and rocks with the Germans behind us. They begin shooting but we hide and the bullets fall above and all round us.

3rd November 1943 — Picinisco (in hiding in Grotto)

Sigbert and I are in a wood. Behind us there is a large rock and the trees all round hide us completely. The sun is beautiful and it is like summer. Sigbert says, 'I want to tell you something. I did not want to tell you before but now I think it is the right moment. Do you remember in Rome last December I received a letter with a handwriting on the envelope that I did not recognise? Well, inside there was another envelope containing the letter. Here it is, I will show it to you.' And he takes the envelopes from his pocket, one inside the other. To my great surprise I see that the letter is from Priscilla! Priscilla's handwriting – what joy! I say, 'Oh, why didn't you tell me before you had received a letter from Priscilla?' — 'Read the letter, and you will see. Fortunately what the letter contains is not true. But it is your fault, little Scheissechen, because you haven't found some possibility to write all this time.'

6th November 1943 — Picinisco (*in hiding in Grotto*)

Oh! My feet are so cold! – so cold that I can't feel them and the pain is so great that I want to cry. Suddenly the train stops and the driver shouts out: 'Half an hour for all those who have got cold feet.' I get out of the train with difficulty but I don't know how to walk because I can't feel my feet. I go into a kitchen and see lots of people drinking boiling coffee in large cups. I tell the maid to bring me some too but she answers rudely that she has not time and that I must find it myself in the cupboard outside. I go to the cupboard which is the same as the one in Via San Martino. I see the two tins of milk but nowhere is there any coffee. I look again under everything but I cannot find the coffee. I go back to the kitchen and say that there is nothing, but no one listens. From outside I hear the train driver shouting. It is time to go back.

*9th November 1943 — Picinisco (**in hiding in Grotto**)*
*Germans everywhere. Along the Fonteduno-Picinisco road
I can see a continual movement of lorries and soldiers. I
am at the Mancinis' house and I can see the square where
there is a great military confusion. I see coming up the hill
towards us a German officer. He is coming towards the
house. I am standing at the gate so I can see him easily. He
has very blond hair and very blue eyes and I know his
smile very well. When he gets close to me I see with great
surprise that it is John.*

*30th November 1943 — Picinisco (**in hiding in Grotto**)*
*We are still hiding from the Germans but we want to find a
better hiding place. Jesus Christ is a high German official
and is enemy number one for us. At all costs we must
avoid being seen by him. We go to the Salstein's house,
hoping we can hide there. Signora Salstein is very friendly
and shakes hands with each one of us twice. She says,
'Now I will call my husband,' but when he comes he says
we must go away immediately if we cannot give him three
tins of Craven A. We go away, and Lewis, Sigbert and I
find ourselves in the Bishop of Chichester's house. The
wife of the latter is very kind to us and says we can safely
hide in the underground passage between their house
and the cathedral. This is a very good idea and we feel
very relieved. She says that first we can eat at the Cellar*

Restaurant so we go towards the lift which is to take us down. But when we are about to leave the room, who do we see pass very rapidly in the corridor, dressed in white, with long blond beard and hair falling on his shoulders, but Jesus Christ! We are very frightened and we wait behind the door. Sigbert says, 'Do you think we are really safe so near to the cathedral?' Lewis says we must take a small risk and I say that at least it will be dark there.

1st December 1943 — Picinisco (in hiding in Grotto)
Lewis, Sigbert and I are hidden in an old hotel in Picinisco. We are living in an unused corner of the old dining room were no one ever enters. There is hardly any room and we sleep one against the other. During the night I get up because I have to go out for a moment. I am dressed in Lewis's pants and white vest. Just outside the hotel I have to pass the Mancinis' house and although it is dark I can see Carlo Alberto sitting at the table in the garden. He laughs and calls me but I pretend not to hear. When I come back he isn't there any more but his maid is leaning out of the window and she is laughing too. In the garden I see a gardener picking up dried sticks and I think how strange it is that life out here goes on as usual while we are sleeping hidden in the dark. But when I enter the Hotel it is not dark any more – and it is not an old unused Hotel any

more. The lights are shining in the dining room, the table is richly laid for five people, and our dirty old blankets are piled up in a heap in the corner. In the centre, talking noisily with Lewis are Edgeworth and Nancy, who have arrived in Italy for the holidays. They are speaking in German with Sigbert. For a moment the proprietor and his wife appear on the scene, both very elegant and they bow to Edge and Nancy. The proprietor says that Nancy is a fascinating little lady, but I think he is a good businessman because Nancy is very fat. We begin to eat, and though Edge and Nancy want to hear all our news, they hardly ever listen when we start telling them. Edgeworth, more blond than ever, turns to me with a broad attractive smile and, winking at me, he says, 'Do you think I am the same as before?' I answer, 'No, I think you are uglier than before.'

4th December 1943 — Picinisco (*in hiding in Grotto*)
I am alone in Max's car. It is a very long time since I have driven a car and I feel very happy. All the windows are open and the air is beautiful. I feel an exhilaration – a kind of intoxication – and I begin to go faster. I press my foot down more and more on the accelerator – always faster, faster. Ah yes! This is magnificent. I watch the speedometer: 40 miles an hour, 50, 60, 70, 75. There is a corner in the road ahead, and a house, but it doesn't matter – it is

lovely to go so fast. I press my foot down still harder – now the house is getting nearer – 80 miles an hour – I can't turn the corner – I can't avoid the house – there is nothing I can do about it – I must hit the house – straight on, straight on — Ah! Now I shut my eyes and I feel the inevitable, terrifically violent shock.

9th December 1943 — Picinisco (in hiding in Grotto)
We go to Rome to fetch some things, and I go immediately to Rosanna. She shows me my clothes, and I notice that the pink silk blouse is very clean. 'Oh,' I say, 'Lots of times I thought of asking you to take it to the cleaners – it was so dirty. Now it is very clean.' 'Yes,' says Rosanna, 'my mother washed it with soap and water – you see it has come out very well. Mother says it is a very fine silk.' I want to put it on at once but I look at myself in the glass and I see that the shoulders which were so well cut and shaped, are now sloping and without any shape. 'It is strange,' I say, 'the shoulders were always the best part of this blouse.' Rosanna says, 'Yes, but my mother has ironed them out flat because it is much nicer.' Then Mrs Moretti comes and confirms what Rosanna has said. 'Yes, it is simpler,' she says. But I am not convinced. It seems that all the shape and smartness are missing. I am very sorry about it because I was very fond of this blouse.

16th December 1943 — Picinisco (in hiding in Grotto)

*I am in a shop in Berlin. Lewis and Sigbert are waiting
outside. I want to buy some fresh 'ricotta' and the woman
in the shop is very kind. She makes me try all the good
things she has to sell, jam with 'ricotta', biscuits, and a
very good chestnut cream. Lewis and Sigbert laugh and
I shout out, 'Don't laugh you two – I am bringing you
something good.' Then the woman gives me some raspberries and says, 'Also for the other two.' Now she is
wrapping up the parcels but she is so slow and talks too
much. She asks me if I know Italy and when I say yes she
tells me that she was born in Picinisco. So we talk about
Picinisco, but I am in a hurry and the parcels are not ready
yet. I don't know how to make her hurry – I say 'yes' and
'no' and look towards the door because I feel that Sigbert
is beginning to get impatient. In fact he looks at his watch
and shouts angrily, 'I didn't say you had to stay inside a
shop for five hours.'*

19th December 1943 — Picinisco (in hiding in Grotto)

*I am in the Mancinis' house and am speaking to Virginia.
Suddenly we hear a German soldier coming, and she is
no more Virginia but Claudette Colbert, dressed in a
beautiful long black velvet dress. She moves gracefully
towards the fireplace and waits quietly. The soldier comes
in and I see at once that it is Conrad Veidt. He goes toward*

her and looking at her in the eyes says, 'You are Countess Yvonne.' For a moment Claudette Colbert's black eyes express fear but she controls herself at once and says in a decisive voice that she is not. 'It is useless to lie,' he says, 'we have all the proofs,' and she cannot protest any more when he takes out of his pocket some old copies of the 'Tatler' and 'Illustrated London News', and he shows her herself many years ago. Page after page are filled with her photographs, with inscriptions below: — 'The beautiful Countess Yvonne at the races.' — 'Young Countess Yvonne with her son.' — 'The charming Countess Yvonne meets Lady X,' etc, etc. She looks at the photographs, then with a resigned air, looks at him, and he says coldly, 'I knew everything. But you shouldn't let your mouth be so hard. You don't seem like a woman anymore. You must let your face be softer,' and then he goes away. When he has gone Claudette Colbert begins to cry. Then an old woman, also dressed in black enters the room, and Claudette runs towards her and still crying throws her arms round the woman's neck. 'Oh, Ursula, we are discovered – dear Ursula, it is the end.' Ursula strokes her forehead and says she will go and make the tea. When the tea is ready Claudette and Ursula have changed back again into Virginia and her old mother-in-law. Virginia, smiling, gives me a cup of boiling tea. I say, 'Do you mind if I give this to Sigbert? He is under the table. We did not want to tell you in order not to embarrass you, but now that the tea has arrived it is a different matter.' Virginia is amused and smiles still more when Sigbert's head and arm emerge from under the table.

19th December 1943 — Picinisco (in hiding in Grotto)
I am walking in a street arm in arm with Eva. We are near Earls Court and pointing to a long street Eva says, 'Perhaps you think you are in the Engadine now?' — 'No', I say, 'I rather think we are about to arrive at Trebovir Road.' Instead, however, we enter a beautiful new perfume shop and Eva says, 'You can buy everything you want to here.' In fact there are many nice small things and I want to buy a lot, especially some soap with a very good scent. Then we go to a book shop (Lacey's) because Eva wants to change a book she borrowed. There I see Barbara Hone and Barbara Longford together. I am about to speak to them but they pass on with just a polite 'Good Morning'. Then we go into South Street because I want to buy a bag of halfpenny buns from Hobbs. Eva waits for me outside the shop, but when I go in I see that Hobbs is no more a cake shop but has changed into a draper's shop – with the same owners and shop girls. I speak to the usual woman with the black hair, 'Why have you changed this shop? Before it was a joy to come here – it was a shop

that one always remembered. Now you only sell lace and ribbons.' She answers, 'Yes, but what can we do? We must think first about business.' Just for the sake of buying something I buy some red cotton and then go out.

4th September 1944 — Rome (after liberation)
I am in my bedroom before breakfast. My daughter comes towards me and says sweetly, 'Come, Mother, it is time for breakfast, let's go down together.' She is a graceful child of ten – and very sweet.

4th September 1944 — Rome (after liberation)
Sigbert and I have arrived in England! We had to leave so quickly and suddenly that I had no time even to dress and I am still in my nightdress with mackintosh on top. We are walking in Piazza San Bernardo and then we go down Via Regina Elena (even though we are in London). Suddenly I see Priscilla and I run towards her shouting, 'Priscilla, Priscilla, we have come back!' Then Max comes and he looks so nice in his blue shirt and rather grey hair. I say, 'Max, Priscilla – here is Sigbert' – but then I suddenly remember that they don't know anything because I have not finished my long letter yet and therefore it has not been posted. Patrick, who arrives at this moment, says, 'I knew – I knew it would happen like this. I told you you would arrive before the letter. Now there is only one thing

to do. You go ahead with Max and Priscilla and tell them everything, Mary.' So I do this and Priscilla says, 'but I know already what you are going to tell us. I have felt it in me for a long time.'

28th September 1944 — Rome (after liberation)

Sigbert and I are on the beach. It is dawn. Everything is grey and misty and the sea is very calm. We are lying on the sand – very, very happy. The beach is deserted and only the birds are flying around – grey and solemn. We are very close to each other and Sigbert is whispering in my ear. I feel all the sweetness that exists and my world is complete. The harmony of our thoughts is so perfect that I don't want to speak – the only words which repeat themselves over and over again in my head are: 'I love you, I love you, I love you.' I almost want to die for happiness – this being the only sublimation further possible. Almost as if he had guessed my thoughts, Sigbert says, 'There is only one thing for us to do – die together – if we die together here in the sea our happiness will continue eternally.' He lifts my head up gently and kisses me. Then he takes my hand and we walk down the beach towards the sea. We enter the water and go slowly out deeper till the water reaches our shoulders. Then we go completely under and try to drown ourselves. I am in Sigbert's arms and we kiss each other and love each other and we can't breathe any more and *the water gurgles round us and we begin to sink, always repeating 'for ever, for ever'.*

22nd October 1944 — Rome (after liberation)
I am about to arrive at South Nore. I am so happy because this is the first time I have seen Max and Mother after all these years. I know that by now they have received my long letter and so they know about Sigbert. I arrive at South Nore and see Mother at once and she kisses me so much and hugs me tightly. 'Oh my darling,' she says and kisses me again. We talk about Sigbert and she understands everything. Then Max comes but he does not notice my joy in seeing him because he passes me as if he had not seen me and also later he does not speak to me. I realise that he is angry and does not understand my situation. How is it possible? Max of all people. I have always been sure that he would have understood every-thing – I was sure of him. It is a great disappointment for me and I am very sad. I go slowly out of the room and outside I meet John who says, 'Come, Mary, I will make you a cup of tea. You are so sad and you need strength.'

16th November 1944 — Rome (after liberation)
Sigbert is seated at a desk in an Allied Office of Infor-mation. I am arranging some flowers in a vase for the desk.

An English officer arrives and he says to me, 'At last I have found you. Don't you remember me?' We sit down on a sofa but really I don't remember who it is. 'Oh,' he says, 'I have known you for a long time – we knew each other when we were children – you were ten, I think. My name is Bob Young, don't you remember?' I think he is probably right but I can't remember anything. He says, 'When will you come to the theatre with me? I am here on leave only for four days.' — 'I don't know,' I answer, 'I will ask Sigbert.' Then I look at Sigbert and see that his face is black with anger and when I go near him he shouts out 'How stupid you are – you think you know everything but you don't understand anything. Don't you see that it is not true that he knows you from before, and that it was only an excuse to speak to you?' He gets up from his chair and looking at me with contempt goes out of the room, and I feel in a very bad temper.

2nd December 1944 Rome — (after liberation)
I am walking along Via Lucullo with a group of other people when suddenly in the street we meet Diana Fawcus. I say, 'Oh! Diana Fawcus.' She smiles a bit timidly but passes on without stopping. I follow her and say, 'Don't you remember me? Mary Gill.' — 'Yes, naturally, but I am here by accident – I ought not to be here.' We arrange to meet at 5.30 when I leave the office, but it seems to me that

she has some mystery because she is acting in a very suspicious way and she is not natural.

22nd December 1944 — Rome (after liberation)
It is half dark – early morning, and in an open field I kill a woman. I take her by the throat and strangle her with my hands. She is lying dead on the ground. I think that no one will discover what I have done because there is no trace, but very soon I am aware that all investigations point against me. I begin to be worried – then frightened, and I think how I can get out of the situation. I try to create some good excuse because I don't want to pass all the rest of my life in prison or be hanged.

26th April 1945 — Rome (after liberation)
Major Gregory telephones me to tell me that he has taken all my luggage to a room behind a hotel. This luggage has been hidden for years and I have not much hope of finding anything intact. I go at once to the hotel and at last find several large packing cases in a rather dark room. I open them all but find nothing interesting till I come to the last case, and there right at the bottom all crushed and ruffled, is Puck! He gets out slowly and stretches his legs and then suddenly becomes all beautiful again as usual – beautiful and furry and round.

OTHER SHORT BOOK TITLES

A Material Girl:
Bess of Hardwick
Kate Hubbard
0-571-20800-2

The Voice of Victorian Sex:
Arthur H. Clough
Rupert Christiansen
0-571-20815-0

Inventor of the Disposable
Culture:
King Camp Gillette
Tim Dowling
0-571-20810-X

Last Action Hero of the
British Empire:
Cdr John Kerans
Nigel Farndale
0-571-20825-8

The Hungarian Who
Walked to Heaven:
Alexander Csoma de Koros
Edward Fox
0-571-20805-3

The Hated Wife:
Carrie Kipling
Adam Nicolson
0-571-20835-5

The Strange World
of Thomas Harris
David Sexton
0-571-20845-2

Funeral Wars
Jonathan Harr
0-571-20850-9

British Teeth
William Leith
0-571-20865-7

Last Drink to to LA
John Sutherland
0-571-20855-X

Your Pedigree Chum
James Langton
0-571-20860-6

Nurse Wolf & Dr Sacks
Paul Theroux
0-571-20840-1